Vision Critical Studies

General Editor: Michael Egan

The Historical Novel and Popular Politics in Nineteenth-century England

Vision Critical Studies published and in preparation:

E. E. Cummings: A Remembrance of Miracles
The Fiction of Sex: Themes and Functions of
Sex Difference in the Modern Novel
Henry James: The Ibsen Years
Margaret Drabble: Puritanism and Permissiveness
The Silent Majority: A Study of the Working
Class in Post-war British Fiction
Wyndham Lewis: Fictions and Satires

George Gissing
The Plays of D. H. Lawrence
Reaching into the Silence: A Study of Eight
Twentieth-century Visionaries

THE HISTORICAL NOVEL AND POPULAR POLITICS IN NINETEENTH-CENTURY ENGLAND

Nicholas Rance

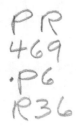

VISION

Vision Press Limited
11–14 Stanhope Mews West
London SW7 5RD

ISBN 0 85478 263 X

Printed in Great Britain
by Clarke, Doble & Brendon Ltd
Plymouth
MCMLXXV

Contents

Editorial Note

Vision Critical Studies will examine mainly nineteenth-century and contemporary imaginative writing, delimiting an area of literary inquiry between, on the one hand, the loose generalities of the "readers' guide" approach and, on the other, the excessively particular specialist study. Crisply written and with an emphasis on fresh insights, the series will gather its coherence and direction from a broad congruity of approach on the part of its contributors. Each volume, based on sound scholarship and research, but relatively free from cumbersome scholarly apparatus, will be of interest and value to all students of the period.

M.E.E.

Acknowledgements

I am grateful to Yale University Library for permission to quote from George Eliot's Journal for 1861 in the Beinecke Rare Book and Manuscript Library, and to Victor Gollancz Ltd. for permission to quote from E. P. Thompson's *The Making of the English Working Class.*

Prefatory Note

The Historical Novel and Popular Politics in Nineteenth-Century England is less comprehensive than the title suggests, and the post-1860s historical novel is not considered, though this omission is not arbitrary. While other authors are discussed in detail, my central interest is in a peculiarly suggestive and significant grouping of historical novels, which the greatest novelists of the day—Dickens, Eliot, Gaskell and Meredith—wrote in the decade preceding the Second Reform Act of 1867. It is a reflection of the mood of their own age that these writers deal with epochs of popular protest and revolution. My introduction and first chapter are about responses to urbanization, attitudes to the past, and the historical novel's development from *Waverley* onwards. Chapter II is concerned with the immediate events, impressions and fears which moulded the historical novels of the late 1850s and 1860s, and associates a renewed seriousness in the historical novel with the rise of the sensation novel. There follow chapters on Dickens' *A Tale of Two Cities*, Eliot's *Romola* and *Felix Holt*, Gaskell's *Sylvia's Lovers*, and Meredith's *Sandra Belloni* and *Vittoria*.

Except that I have used the Oxford Illustrated Dickens, and unless otherwise stated, all references to the novels are to first editions.

My great debt is to the encouragement and many invaluable suggestions of John Goode, of Reading University. Juliet Mitchell, late of Reading University, has also helped and inspired me, and I am very grateful to her, too.

I have much appreciated the typing of Sue Goddard, a member of the Psychology Department at Reading University.

N.A.R.
July, 1974

8

"The objection to historical romance is that so few men are fit to write it. It is the most ambitious and the most difficult, because the most complete, manner of solving the historical problem."

The Saturday Review, 11 September, 1858

"The wealthy pay little heed to the change which is taking place in the habits of thought of the million; but when they read of strike after strike for increased wages, of prolonged conflicts between masters and men, and of the enormous development of the trades-union system, they begin to inquire about their own security, and almost to wish for a return to the blessed days when squires knew little, and shopkeepers knew less, and working people knew nothing at all."

The Pall Mall Gazette, 19 July, 1866

Introduction

The City and the Past

When Lucy Snowe, the heroine of Charlotte Brontë's *Villette* (1853), comes to London for the first time, she has no taste for the languid West End, but is exhilarated by the bustle of the City, and her deep excitement is as pervasive in Dickens' descriptions of London life as any sense of individual isolation. Nevertheless, the character arriving in London and feeling alone in the crowd was a theme of Victorian fiction. Between 1700 and 1820, the population of London nearly doubled, from 674,000 to 1,274,000; it was 1,873,000 in 1841 and 4,232,000 in 1891. The populations of the new northern industrial towns were multiplying still more rapidly from the mid-eighteenth century. Bradford grew from 13,000 to 104,000 between 1800 and 1861, and by then, for the first time anywhere, rural inhabitants were in a minority in England. The prolific historical romancer, G. P. R. James, set his *Henry Masterton; or, The Adventures of a Young Cavalier* (1832) in the Civil War years. Henry Masterton reflects of his early experience of London that

> of all kinds of solitude, there is none like the solitude of a great town—so utterly desert, as far as human sympathies go. A great town is like an immense Eastern bazaar, where men buy and sell and are bought and sold; and without one has some merchantable quality or commodity, or some of the many kinds of coin with which the trade in human relationships is carried on, he is like a beggar in the market-place, and it must be all sterile as the plains of Arabia Petraea.

The capital's tumultuous expansion dated from the end of the sixteenth century, and London was most liable to oppress by its magnitude in the seventeenth: James need not be accused of projecting a modern response on to his cavalier. But in *Henry Master-*

11

ton, the Civil War is powerless to dissipate the golden haze with which James envelops the past. It is significant and typical that the hero's coming to London should be unique in the novel in evoking intense feeling.

The fear and repulsion inspired by the city are integrally related to the rise of the novel, and apparent in Richardson's work, but the industrial revolution inaugurated "the age of great cities", exposing social divisions which became subtler and more absolute during the nineteenth century. In his introduction to *Culture and Society*, Raymond Williams traces the ramifications of the word "class":

> it is only at the end of the eighteenth century that the modern structure of *class*, in its social sense, begins to be built up. First comes *lower classes*, to join *lower orders*, which appears earlier in the eighteenth century. Then, in the 1790s, we get *higher classes*; *middle classes* and *middling classes* follow at once; *working classes* in about 1815; *upper classes* in the 1820s. *Class prejudice, class legislation, class consciousness, class conflict*, and *class war* follow in the course of the nineteenth century.

In *The Condition of the Working Class in England in 1844* (1845), Engels is scathing about bourgeois writers lamenting the growth of cities as an evil, as though they were solely responsible for the divisions which they revealed. A more radical evasion was to accept the isolation felt in the city as illuminating the human condition. Already, in Book VII of *The Prelude* (1799–1805), such was Wordsworth's response to London, and by the 1850s, as urban life imposed itself as the norm, his response was widely shared. The mystification of the present implied that of the past, and it is in this context that the historical novels of the 1850s and 1860s, including those by Dickens, Eliot, Gaskell and Meredith, from *A Tale of Two Cities* in 1859 to *Felix Holt* and *Vittoria* in 1866, must be examined.

Georg Lukacs has suggested that 1848 marked a watershed in the manner in which writers viewed society. After the June Days, they had either to affirm or reject a socialist ideology connected with the industrial proletariat, and those rejecting the new perspectives made themselves apologists for a declining capitalism. In England as well as France, the working class was emerging as an independent force, and becoming increasingly organised, if less

12

radical, after the extinction of Chartism. Remarking that the changed social consciousness of post-1848 literature in England cannot definitively be related to the events of that year, John Goode has shown in his essay, "1848 and the Strange Disease of Modern Love", "that, in a general way, the despair, hysteria or mystification which appears in so much of the literature of the mid-Victorian period is encapsulated in works which respond to the Revolutions".[1] 1848 is a significant date in the development of the historical novel, since it was then that Bulwer, whose mission was to reincarnate the great characters of history, published his last romance, *Harold*. In the succeeding years, historical novelists lacked self-assurance, and most heroes became private individuals, with their own private history, rather than great men. Despair of recapturing the past is voiced in some novels of the 1850s, notably Thackeray's, and on a wide scale, certainly by the 1860s, the attempt is abandoned.

The Revolutions seem to have accelerated, without initiating, a tendency among English writers to detach themselves from the historical process. Thackeray is a novelist whose response to the events of 1848 is on record. He approved Fitzjames Stephen's remarks on "Liberalism" in the *Cornhill* in 1862: "the article is a very moderate sensible plea for an aristocratic government, and shows the dangers of a democracy quite fairly. . . . The politics of gentlemen are pretty much alike. Since '48 in France, and especially since America, I for one am very much inclined to subscribe to Stephen's article." But there were more immediate pressures, and as early as *Catherine* (1839–40), his novel of criminal life in the eighteenth century, he clung to a protective fatalism: "some call the doctrine of destiny a dark creed; but, for me, I would fain try and think it a consolatory one". It was in the 1830s in England that nostalgia became a prevailing impulse, when the morally and physically degraded workers, thronged in cities which could not accommodate them, and, in the industrial north, acquiring a mass identity, aroused the consternation of the other classes. Asa Briggs mentions the "lively brew" resulting from the blend between political radicalism and labour economics in the early 1830s, and refers to a communication of Peter Gaskell's to Lord

[1] *Literature and Politics in the Nineteenth Century*, 1971, p. 47.

Melbourne in 1834: "since the Steam Engine has concentrated men into particular localities—has drawn together the population into dense masses—and since an imperfect education has enlarged, and to some degree distorted their views, union is become easy and from being so closely packed, simultaneous action is readily excited'.[2] Dickens resisted and analysed the lure of a retrospective escapism, and from *Oliver Twist* (1837–38) onwards, was engaged with the conditions giving rise to a hardening of feeling between and within classes. But in 1829, in "Signs of the Times", Carlyle combined a bitter attack on *laissez-faire* with a wariness of the urban masses, and a depreciation of the intrinsic significance of popular protest. His history of the *French Revolution* (1837) displays the tendencies which Lukacs ascribes to the post-1848 reaction: Carlyle abstracts himself from a history which is regarded as spectacle, madness and fever-frenzy running their course.

Georg Lukacs, who takes *Salammbô* (1862) as representative of the post-1848 trends in the historical novel, quotes Flaubert's remark: "few will guess how sad one had to be to resuscitate Carthage!" In the 1830s in England, the Middle Ages became charged with emotion, and on a popular level, the 1830s and 1840s are the boom years of the historical romance, generally dealing with a remote past beyond embodiment. Of course, a shaming contrast with the nineteenth century was the point of much medievalism, but there was no serious attempt to show how the present had evolved from an idealised past. Tocqueville asked in 1835 (in the first volume of *Democracy in America*) how credible it was that the democracy which had "annihilated the feudal system, and vanquished kings", would "respect the citizen and the capitalist". Carlyle, like Ruskin, was as apprehensive of democracy as he was antagonistic to *laissez-faire*, and could not relate his proposals for change to the progressive forces within his own society, only to a past whose main feature was its dissimilarity with the present.

Associating the novel's rise with that of the city, Ian Watt comments:

> an environment so large and various that only a little of it can be experienced by any one individual, and a system of values that

[2] *Essays in Labour History*, 1967, p. 63.

is mainly economic—these have combined to provide the novel in general with two of its most characteristic themes. . . .[3]

In the interpolated tale in *Tom Jones* (1749), the Man of the Hill flees to London to enjoy the anonymity guaranteed by urban crowds, but learns that "a man may be as easily starved to death in Leadenhall-market as in the deserts of Arabia". Tom Jones finds that the social orders in the capital are segregated, and economic values colour his relations with Lady Bellaston, which are described as "commerce". The new capitalist, Mr Nightingale the elder, is bent on selling his son in marriage to the highest bidder, and believes that worth attaches to nothing but money. Without compassion, the rich elevate the act of giving above the recipient; and this interpretation of charity, depending on the prolongation of class divisions, anticipates the view which by Blake's time is well established, that "Pity would be no more,/If we did not make somebody Poor". In the 1740s, the hypocrisy is more readily available to exposure: Tom is naive in his compliment to the masked Lady Bellaston at the ball—"sure, madam, you must have infinite discernment to know people in all disguises". Matthew Arnold was to show his own generation as "trick'd in disguises". The difference is that "The Buried Life" (1852) is a personal cry of despair, since Arnold, too, is a victim and feels society as all-conditioning. Fielding, while not idealising the countryside, can still afford to adopt the stance of the detached commentator on London vice.

The poetry of Goldsmith and Cowper stresses estrangement between the social orders in towns and cities, rather than the way in which the personal relations of the monied classes reflect the new economic values. The pastoral bias of *The Deserted Village* (1770) and *The Task* (1784) diverted attention from the precise quality of life in the towns. Nevertheless, these poems are not innocently pastoral. Rousseau, whose works are scattered with diatribes on the city, dislikes cities because they are crowded and also because of visible oppression; and Goldsmith and Cowper, too, are concerned with the expanding gulf between rich and poor as well as overcrowding. Goldsmith hopes that his poetry will "teach erring man to spurn the rage of gain", and

[3] *The Rise of the Novel*, 1957, p. 180.

points to the contrasts which rage for gain is producing in the cities. Writing against "luxury", he gives a garish description of the town and its pleasures, but the luxury is that of the few, who exploit the many. The "trade" ruining the countryside and desolating Sweet Auburn is also desolating the urban poor. The riot and incontinence of London lead Cowper to the pastoral platitude, "God made the country, and man made the town", but he is alert to what is happening in the city, and London's "crowded coop" is split by divisions of class.

The pastoral sentiment of Dickens' characters is linked with callous evasion, or schizophrenia, and forbidden to his readers: in *Bleak House* (1852–53), Chesney Wold and Lincoln's Inn Fields exude duplicity and decay. Blake associates pastoral with innocence, and both are shadowed by the experience of a political and economic system marking lives in country and town alike. It was in the 1790s in England that men of property, alarmed by Radical agitation, began to regard the poor as the "masses", but in the *Songs of Experience* of 1794, Blake made manifest the social connections beneath the mystification. The "marriage hearse" of "London" is literally blighted. Men incited to barbarism by the economic orthodoxy have compensated by idealising their wives: the fleshy woman is sought among London's prostitutes, recruited through the conditions of modern marriage.

With less sense of the determining power complex, Wordsworth presents a similar vision of the city. As in Blake, what is apparent is division within and between classes, and in the individual mind, in *The Prelude*, Wordsworth compares his response to London with his experience of first hearing a woman blaspheme, when he

> shuddered, for a barrier seemed at once
> Thrown in, that from humanity divorced
> Humanity, splitting the race of man
> In twain, yet leaving the same outward form.

Amongst the urban crowd, "that huge fermenting mass of humankind", the poet reflects that "the face of every one/That passes by me is a mystery!" For Wordsworth, the mystery is emblematic, and his blind beggar, unknown and unseeing, is Everyman as well as the individual in the crowd.

16

Cobbett's change of heart in his old age illustrates the progress from moralistic criticism of the city as such (and as destructive of country life) towards a sophisticated analysis of class structures within the city. In his own 1830 edition of *Rural Rides*, Cobbett customarily described London as the great Wen. He did not die until 1835, and the enlarged edition produced by his son shows how Cobbett became more discriminating, and began to extend to the urban proletariat the sympathy he felt for agricultural labourers. He wrote that there was

> no hope of any change for the better but from the working people. The farmers will sink to a very low state; and thus the Thing (barring accidents) may go on, until neither farmer nor tradesman will see a joint of meat on his table once in a quarter of a year. It appears likely to be precisely as it was in France. . . .

The "Thing", the capital system, whose operations in the countryside he had always acutely registered, is now seen as oppressing "all those who do not share in the taxes", and the "Wen", the city, has ceased to excite enmity.

In his *Confessions of an English Opium Eater* (1822), De Quincey wrote that sometimes during his travels by night in London, he

> came suddenly upon such knotty problems of alleys, alleys without soundings, such enigmatical entries, and such sphinx's riddles of streets without obvious outlets or thoroughfares, as must baffle the audacity of porters, and confound the intellects of hackney coachmen. I could almost have believed, at times, that I must be the first discoverer of some of these *terrae incognitae*, and doubted whether they had yet been laid down in the modern charts of London.

The tormenting dreams of his later years were De Quincey's price for his excursions, and the revelations of a London life hidden from more respectable citizens. Dickens also wandered London by night, as much an explorer as those seeking the source of the Nile, which was no more remote than the slums for most of his readers. Contemporary poets, and most notably Matthew Arnold, gave anguished expression to the theme of isolation in the city. The "buried life" finds an outlet only in personal relations, and the beloved hand laid in ours is opposed to the interminable "rush and glare" of work in the city, where men are "alien to the rest/Of men, and alien to themselves". And "A Summer Night" (1852), the other poem in which Arnold writes about living in London, anticipates the central image of *Little Dorrit* (1855–57), stating that "most men in a brazen prison live". When Tennyson dealt with the city, his revulsion was as great as Arnold's. But that the city featured so little in their poetry is more significant than the few urban poems which they did produce. In the dreamy medievalising of *Idylls of the King*, whose first four books appeared in 1859, the past was too innocent to have bred fears of democracy and revolution.

Engels, in 1845, saw the crowded city as the starkest revelation of the essence of an organised capitalist economy: "the dissolution of mankind into monads, of which each one has a separate principle and a separate purpose, is here carried out to its utmost extreme". The city was increasingly seen as a revelation of the human condition. The isolation which is first experienced as a disturbing novelty is then rationalised, and reflections on the mystery of life are commonplace in mid-Victorian novels and histories. The fourth volume of Froude's *History of England from the Fall of Wolsey to the Death of Elizabeth* (1856–70) appeared in 1858, and began by suggesting the dilemma facing historians.

> Whoever has attended but a little to the phenomena of human nature has discovered how inadequate is the clearest insight which he can hope to attain into character and disposition. Every one is a perplexity to himself and a perplexity to his neighbours; and men who are born in the same generation, who are exposed to the same influences, trained by the same teachers, and live from childhood to age in constant and familiar intercourse, are often little more than shadows to each other, intelligible in superficial form and outline, but divided inwardly by impalpable and mysterious barriers.

Froude proceeds to argue from the obscurity of the present to the still greater dimness of the receding vistas of the past.

> And if from those whom we daily meet, whose features are before our eyes, and whose minds we can probe with questions, we are nevertheless thus divided, how are the difficulties of the understanding increased when we are looking back from another age, with no better assistance than books, upon men who played

their parts upon the earth under other outward circumstances, with other beliefs, other habits, other modes of thought, other principles of judgment!

This is only the most forthright statement of misgivings which shadow Froude's enterprise. In 1856, the *Westminster* reviewer of the first two volumes echoed Froude's sentiments on the past, while disclosing that what he, with Froude, took to be "the phenomena of human nature", were also social and urban phenomena:

> it requires but a minute's reflection for any one who traverses the streets of a great city, to perceive how slight his knowledge is of his contemporaries; and the further we go back from the present the less clear is our vision.

"An impassable gulf" divides present from past, which appears moribund; so that the *National*, reviewing Froude, writes of history as a "pageant which we can resuscitate". Commenting in 1857 on the first volume of Buckle's *History of Civilization in England*, Mark Pattison in the *Westminster Review* termed history "that shifting quicksand", and compared the intellectual gratification of reading Grote or Michelet with that excited by a superior novel. The reader is perpetually conscious that the historian's characters are "beings of his own creation, and that the next enchanter who arises will attach the same names, and ascribe the same fortunes, to a quite different set of spiritual creations".

The present's prehistory was taken as random, and accounts of the past derived consistency only from the historian's own emotions and prejudices. Carlyle admitted as much, despite his pleas for conscientious research. The validity and necessity of modernisation was a welcome principle to those who, theoretically denying that the past might be conveyed, still had views which they wanted to publicise. Middle-class historians and historical novelists tended to warn against revolutions, which were inevitably disastrous, since the masses in history were tools manipulated either by the demagogue or, with more sophistication, the *zeitgeist*, imposed from above and obviating research.

Though Engels, writing of Manchester, records the systematic concealment of working-class misery and squalor from "the eyes of wealthy gentlemen and ladies with strong stomachs and weak nerves", it would be misleading to suggest that the mystery of the great city was not genuinely felt by the upper and middle classes. While advocating the passing of the 1867 Reform Bill, *The Times* still remarked just before the Bill became law that the nation was "taking a leap in the dark". But subjectivism helped the conservative cause: if the city was a mystery, reflecting the human condition, then the condition of the masses was nobody's fault, and there was no call for the remorse which weighed on De Quincey, as he rambled the *terrae incognitae* of London. With a clear conscience, the monied classes might defend their interests. Although the *Westminster* reviewer illustrates Froude's human mystery by reference to city life, that life is bleakly assumed, and where Arnold juxtaposes estrangement and an evasive remedy, Blake had analysed estrangement in the city in terms of economics and power.

The mystery engulfing urban life and the past was genuinely felt, but also genuinely comforting. R. H. Hutton, writing in 1859 on "The Religion of the Working Classes", described Chartism, socialism and revolution as "misdirected religious cravings", and pronounced history's universal lesson to be that "such evil as there is, is within us". Lady Bellaston, at the ball, recognised her acquaintances through their masks, though Tom did not know her: a century later, there was less curiosity to see what could be seen.

Interpretations of Past and Present

Maria Edgeworth's *Castle Rackrent* (1800) purported to be a narration by the old steward of the eccentricities and ruin of a family of Irish landlords in the eighteenth century. This was the first novel on the past to relate character, and not merely costume, to the particular age; and Scott paid handsome tribute. In the Postscript to *Waverley*, he wrote that he had intended to describe his countrymen, "not by a caricatured and exaggerated use of the national dialect, but by their habits, manners, and feelings; so as, in some distant degree, to emulate the admirable Irish portraits drawn by Miss Edgeworth. . . ." The compliment was deserved, but Scott was too modest, and obscured his own originality. *Castle Rackrent* is celebrating the death of Ireland's past, and Maria Edgeworth regards her characters as curiosities. Nations, like individuals, she writes in the preface, "can bear to be rallied for their past follies and absurdities, after they have acquired new habits and a new consciousness". Scott, on the other hand, saw the past as the vital prehistory of his own age. *Waverley*, the first genuine historical novel, was begun in 1805, put aside for seven years, and published in 1814.

Many ballad-collections since Bishop Percy's first volume of 1765 had manifested an interest in the people in history, and the thirteen-year-old Scott was entranced by discovering *Reliques of Ancient English Poetry*, though his own sense of the past was more immediate than a gentlemanly antiquarianism. His conscious values were typically Augustan, but in breaking away from the conventions of eighteenth-century literature to write for and about a much broader community, he was sharing in the Romantic response to changed conditions. The Romantic poets and Scott lived in the years when Britain moved from an economy of agriculture and domestic handicrafts to become "the workshop of the world". From the 1780s onwards, an unprecedented industrial and technological development was visibly gathering momentum, and actuality belied the standards and fixed categories of the eighteenth-century ruling class. The rise of industry coincided with that of democracy, and the French Revolution, inspiring the Romantic poets by its example, gave direction to Radical discontent in England. In *Lyrical Ballads* (1798), Wordsworth eschewed an artificial poetic diction to record in "language really used by men" the affairs of the common people, whose lives were being transformed by economic forces, reducing Margaret's cottage to ruin and letting Michael's estate fall into a stranger's hand. Following Maria Edgeworth, whose *Castle Rackrent* was composed at the same time as *Lyrical Ballads*, Scott wrote on his national history from a popular point of view. Previously, only a ruling-class outlook on the past had been expressed in novels.

Scott declares in the Postscript to *Waverley* that "there is no European nation which, within the course of half a century, or little more, has undergone so complete a change as this kingdom of Scotland". Economically, as well as politically, Scotland was backward, and though Scottish engineers contributed importantly to the Industrial Revolution, they had to work in England. But what Scott referred to as "the gradual influx of wealth and extension of commerce", and improved communications which sacrificed regional character to the primacy of London, perfected the transformation begun by the violent aftermath to his theme in *Waverley*, the Jacobite rebellion of 1745. The power of the Highland chiefs and legal authority of the Lowland nobility were brought to an end, and the entire Jacobite party, which had been sternly separatist in maintaining Scottish manners and customs, was wiped out. By the early nineteenth century, the old Scotland was near extinction, persisting in antiquarian studies and Scott's own Jacobite relics at Abbotsford. His countrymen were all the more conscious of their national identity in the past, and Scott wrote *Waverley*, he remarks in the Postscript, to record that identity before the memory faded. The Scottish people in 1814 are "a class of beings as different from their grandfathers, as the existing English are from those of Queen Elizabeth's time", but the novelist did not feel about the generation of 1745 what Froude was to feel about the Elizabethans. Conscious of difference in the past, Scott saw that an analysis of the difference was necessary to interpret the present: "like those who drift down the stream of a deep and smooth river, we are not aware of the progress we have made until we fix our eye on the now-distant point from which we have been drifted".

Like Jane Austen's, Scott's response to nature was more Augustan than Wordsworthian. Even the austere beauty of the Highlands might be reconciled with human improvement, so that in *Waverley*, Flora MacIvor's planting of trees and shrubs, on the borders of a lake, "added to the grace, without diminishing the romantic wildness of the scene". Scott's formulated views on history also belonged to the eighteenth century, and he alludes confidently to "passions common to men in all stages of society": only a "necessary colouring" is cast upon these passions by manners and laws in a particular age. The depiction in the novel of contrasting social states would, Scott hoped, "vary and . . . illustrate the moral lessons" which he was bent on instilling.

On the other hand, Scott could justify a preoccupation with past politics by claiming that the action of *Waverley* depended on motives which "necessarily arose from the feelings, prejudices,

and parties of the time". Through direct inspection and embodiment of the popular life ignored by accredited historians, the
novelist exposed their platitudes. The next generation of historical novelists did not proceed beyond mulling over the example
in prefaces, and in his own works on the distant past, Scott was
prone to write court history through default. The popular life
of the epoch had to be known before it was rendered, and Louis XI
in *Quentin Durward* (1823) is a dominating presence and a
history-maker. But in the novels dealing with Scotland since the
seventeenth century, the great men are minor characters. Here,
as Georg Lukacs remarks generally of Scott, he "lets his important
figures grow out of the being of the age, he never explains the
age from the position of its great representatives".

Scott followed Maria Edgeworth in reflecting in the destiny of a
hero with mixed allegiances the turning-points of history. *The
Heart of Midlothian* (1818) has a strong heroine rather than a
vacillating hero, but Donald Davie has convincingly argued that
the use of the divided family involves Scott in difficulties. Effie
must be hopelessly weak to counterbalance Jeanie's strength, and
her weakness cannot be defined or explained. Waverley, as waver-
ing as his name suggests, allows Scott to portray Hanoverians
and Jacobites alike with insight and sympathy. But Scott set an
unfortunate precedent in assuming the existence of the typical
Waverley hero. Writing anonymously in the *Quarterly Review* in
1817, he dismissed his heroes as "very amiable and very insipid
sort of young men", and suggested why they should be. "We
think that we can perceive that this error is also in some degree
occasioned by the dramatic principle upon which the author frames
his plots. His chief characters are never actors, but always acted
upon by the spur of circumstances, and have their fates uniformly
determined by the agency of the subordinate persons." These
sentences are a revelation of the deliberate artistry which Scott
was wary of admitting, but do not account for the success of
Waverley or, indeed, the failure of *Rob Roy* (1817). The vacilla-
tion of the hero had itself to be historically motivated. Though
the Scottish novels with settings ranging from the late seventeenth century of *Old Mortality* to the last years of the eighteenth
in *The Antiquary* are sometimes implied to be of equal merit,
Scott's version of events earlier than the 1730s tends to owe more

23

to his gentlemanly preconceptions than his familiarity. Donald Davie remarks that the hero of *Rob Roy*, Francis Osbaldistone, is anachronistic as a man of feeling in 1715. The historical novel turns to romance to accommodate his insubstantiality, and while his character, in so far as he has one, is similar to Waverley's, only Osbaldistone wearies the reader.

Waverley belongs to the 1740s, when the man of feeling was emerging. The novel concludes with a dedication to Henry Mackenzie, and Flora MacIvor predicts Waverley's destiny: to bask "in the quiet circle of domestic happiness, lettered indolence, and elegant enjoyments, of Waverley-Honour". Flora even alludes to his refitting the library "in the most exquisite Gothic taste", in 1745 an anachronistic prophecy, but relating Waverley's fortunes to those of his class at a particular time, when the past could safely be treated as bizarre and amusing. Like Waverley, the heroines of the successful historical novels of the 1860s look backwards and forwards, and their divided allegiance is rooted in history. In Mrs Gaskell's *Sylvia's Lovers*, set in the 1790s, Sylvia is drawn both by the feckless spontaneity attaching to traditional pursuits, like farming and whaling, and by commercial respectability; while Meredith's Vittoria in 1848 fluctuates between the attitudes of the middle class which has nurtured her in England, and those of the Italian revolutionaries.

In Shelley's poem, written in 1812 at the age of eighteen, the fairy Queen Mab conveys "in just perspective to the view" the events

> Of old and wondrous times
> Which dim tradition interruptedly
> Teaches the credulous vulgar. . . .

The best Waverley novels are an objective portrayal of Scottish history of the eighteenth century, whose characters are comprehensible in their own terms. Compared with early and mid-Victorian medievalists, Scott did not look at the remote past with misty eyes. His Saxons and Normans were endowed with the passions common to men throughout history, and he deflates the sentimental view of medieval chivalry. We are told that the twelfth-century days of *Ivanhoe* (1819) "are not the days of King Arthur": they are certainly not the days of Tennyson's King

Arthur. But their successful embodiment was out of the question, and the impulse behind the medieval novels was escapist. We gain no insights into the passing of feudalism from Scott, who is uncritical of the medieval social structure. In the nineteenth century, mystifications of the historical process emanated from men otherwise forced to see themselves as characters in history, and extend the same credit to past generations. The alternative responses to rapid change were combined in Scott.

Eighteenth-century historians had thought the Middle Ages barren of memorable events, and had undertaken to convey whole epochs in a sentence or paragraph. Curt dismissals of medieval times, with a grudging tolerance extended to the twelfth century and later, persisted into the nineteenth: Enlightenment attitudes dominated English historiography until the 1830s. "We begin in darkness and calamity," wrote Henry Hallam of his *A View of the State of Europe during the Middle Ages* (1818), "and though the shadows grow fainter as we advance, yet we are to break off our pursuit as the morning breathes upon us, and the twilight reddens into the lustre of day." The Renaissance was the rebirth of classical culture, and also of history, following an obscure era of barbarity and superstition. From the 1760s, the Gothic novel flourished and Gothic ruins were appreciated. But for writers like Horace Walpole, who made Strawberry Hill into "a little Gothic castle", and William Beckford, who commissioned the ruins of Fonthill Abbey, the characteristics of Gothic were gloom, wildness and fear. Supposedly, medieval man shared the nature of his eighteenth-century counterpart, and it was because the Middle Ages were natural that the fascination they exerted was legitimate. In the nineteenth century, on the other hand, the Middle Ages fascinated because they seemed so different from modern life.

Though Scott's best work inspired others to write on the crucial prehistory of their own age, his medieval novels were generally imitated, and the great majority of the historical novels of the nineteenth century were set in the distant past, especially in Rome or the Middle Ages. The novelists were privileged in the same way as the various medievalising movements: where little was known, history was what one made it. Too removed from the age to perceive its motivating forces, they found themselves writing the kind of history in which they wished to believe. Events were interpreted in the light of an unchanging human nature, with great men as history-makers, while characters who did not move in a solid environment enacted parables comforting to Victorians. *Romola*, set in Renaissance Florence, demonstrated the futility of political reform in the 1860s: Ruskin's version of the "nature of Gothic" was an important influence here and also in *Felix Holt*, dealing with the 1830s. The Middle Ages in fiction were either absolutely remote from contemporary life, in the sense that modernised heroes and heroines breathed a romantic "period" atmosphere, or else, more cunningly, the concept of the enduring English-Saxon character, resistant to Norman and Stuart tyranny, endowed readers with the spirit of the free Saxons. There was no hint of a gradual but progressive development from medieval times to the present.

The title of Carlyle's *Past and Present* (1843) suggests a sense of historical change, but not of historical process. Looking back to the Elizabethans, Froude was conscious of their difference from his contemporaries, conscious of change, but had no sense of organic relation between past and present. Paradoxically, the amateurish enthusiasm for the Middle Ages was symptomatic of the generalised estrangement from a past evolving the Victorian present. By the mid-nineteenth century, historians knew that there was more to be said of the years between the barbarian invasions and the fifteenth century than that they were shrouded in darkness; but the medieval period was still the most neglected by accredited historians of the English past when Stubbs began publishing his *Constitutional History* in 1874. The very sparseness of information conveying the Middle Ages to the Victorians was conducive to visions of the good society, and while there was an intense awareness of the difference between medieval times and the nineteenth century, that was most intelligibly explained by a fall from grace into the modern world. The divisions of Victorian society might be lamented without compunction, and even such stern critics as Carlyle and Ruskin, who did not altogether idealise the Middle Ages, diluted their prophecy by reference to the past, whence came their remedies.

*   *   *

26

J. H. Newman remembered Scott in his prayers as the man who, through popularising the medieval past, had made possible the religious revival in England. From the 1830s, all renderings of the Middle Ages were coloured by the Oxford Movement; Carlyle harked back to the age of faith in *Past and Present*. In *Bleak House* (1852–53), Dickens is bitter about the Puseyite dandies who gather at Chesney Wold, Sir Leicester Dedlock's place in Lincolnshire, to lament the vulgar's want of faith in things in general—things, Dickens adds, which have long been discredited. Newman and his immediate associates were impatient of gothicising, but the restoration of the Catholic trappings of church furniture, though of central importance only to a minority, reflected the movement's inspiration. The Oxford Movement was an attempt to revive the power and prestige which had once attached to the Church, but was vanishing in the nineteenth century. Charles X of France, who wished to restore the Church's medieval pre-eminence and to punish sacrilege by death, had been forced to abdicate. In England, the Swing Riots spurred Hurrell Froude to complain that "the labouring population, as well as the farmers, seem thoroughly indifferent to the welfare of the parsons and squires". Since Roman Catholic Emancipation in 1829, there had been agitation from those who identified the bishops with Toryism, and resented the abuses which the Church perpetuated. The Bishop of Bristol's palace was burnt down when the Lords rejected reform in 1831. Meanwhile, a Whig government seemed bent on truckling to the utilitarian spirit of the age. Lord Grey had told the bishops resisting reform that they should set their own house in order before concerning themselves with politics; a hint denounced by Keble as Erastianism of the worst order.

The Tractarians regarded and defended the Church not as a state establishment, but as the Divine Society founded by Christ. They were indifferent to the great issues which many thought to bear on the contemporary role of the Church. Souls of the poor were presumed to benefit through poverty and subjection; and Newman, wondering why there were radical politicians, concluded that they were offspring of the fallen angels. The immediate provocation of Keble's Assize Sermon, which inaugurated the Oxford Movement in 1833, was the introduction of a bill to suppress ten Irish bishoprics. The conditions which made the eventual disestablishment of the Irish Church inevitable were beside the point. To deprive the Apostolical Church of Christ in Ireland of her worldly goods was sacrilege; as it would be in England. Most of those who supported Keble had as little grasp of theology as of the Irish situation, but were alarmed for their own security and prospects. Like Sir Leicester Dedlock, whose own enthusiasm for the Middle Ages would have been qualified by the memory of Wat Tyler, they feared that the floodgates had opened; and if so, heroic exertions were required to stem the tide.

In *Past and Present* (1843), Carlyle criticised historians, writing in the tradition of the Enlightenment, for too glibly despising "absurd superstitious blockheads of Monks", and remarked that since only chaos and fanaticism were seen in the past, it might comfortably be assumed that the turmoil of the present reflected an inevitable state of affairs. Here was an example of the mechanistic thinking which Carlyle was bent on undermining, and his insistence that the England of 1200 was not "peopled with mere vaporous Fantasms", but was "a green solid place, that grew corn and several other things", went naturally with his inquiring how, in the nineteenth century, the ritual dogmas of *laissez-faire* shaped the lives of the dumb millions.

If Carlyle had viewed the Middle Ages nostalgically, that would have been a mechanical response to his opponents, but he was not pleading for medievalism in the nineteenth century, and was more sceptical than some of his contemporaries. His twelfth century is less idyllic than Ruskin's Gothic era, or Disraeli's image of the Middle Ages in *Coningsby* and *Sybil*, where the dissolution of the monasteries was regarded as a calamitous and unprovoked evil. Carlyle did not blame Henry VIII for the dissolution, and recognised traces of monastic corruption as early as the twelfth century. There were game-laws and other grinding injustices in the Middle Ages and, not surprisingly, frequent insurrections. But, wrote Carlyle (eschewing the myth of the Norman Yoke), though enthralled by Cedric the Saxon, Gurth "had the inexpressible satisfaction of feeling himself related indissolubly, though in a rude brass-collar way, to his fellow-mortals in this Earth". The traditional loyalties of a society where rank assumed it responsibilities, and the serf was entitled to the parings of his master's pig, had vanished with feudalism, and the nineteenth century had spawned only the "enlightened Egoism" of atomised individuals, prone to the morbid introspection which Carlyle associated with Methodism, or the vacuous self-assertion of Puseyism:

> that certain human souls, living on this practical Earth, should think to save themselves and a ruined world by noisy theoretic demonstrations and laudations of *the* Church, instead of some un-noisy, unconscious, but *practical*, total, heart-and-soul demonstrations of *a* Church: this, in the circle of revolving ages, this also was a thing we were to see.

There was no serfdom in the nineteenth century, but the freedom equated with *laissez-faire* was, for the workers, only the freedom to starve. New loyalties and bonds had to be forged. The age must find appropriate heroes, a working aristocracy such as the twelfth century possessed and revered, to replace the "Millocracy", steeped in mammonism, and the idle aristocracy, ruinous to the country and itself.

The exposure by contrast of the social consequences of *laissez-faire* was distinct from Tennyson's fascination with a changeless order outside the historical process. Carlyle's appeal for strong government is more suspect in his later writings than in *Past and Present*, where we know the heroic charge: to dispel the utilitarian egoism reducing workers to hands, and guarantee them the fair wage of food and warmth enjoyed by the Saxon serf. But even in *Past and Present*, the invocation of heroes distracted Carlyle from a radical analysis of modern conflict; and so did the framework of allusion, highly selective for all his concessions, to the twelfth century and heroic Abbot Samson. The model society was found in a past which, emphatically, there was no reviving, but Carlyle could think of improvement in the present only in terms of re-storation.

The Young England movement did not contribute to the practical politics of the nineteenth century, and Disraeli, at least, seems to have retained a sense of the fanciful nature of Young England policies. They were forgotten as soon as he had ousted Peel and achieved a position of power within the Conservative party, and neither Disraeli's promotion of the 1867 Reform

Bill, nor the social reforms of 1875–76, derived from the Tory
Democracy which he had advocated in the 1840s. Like Ruskin's
later suggestion of entrusting the functions of capitalists to guilds,
Disraeli's invocation of that simpler and more harmonious society,
his image of the Middle Ages, manifested a wish to re-establish
contact with the potentially revolutionary workers, and to escape
the complexities of Victorian civilisation. In *Coningsby* (1844) and
Sybil (1845), both Gothic architecture and Catholicism were
treated respectfully, though the Roman Church was harshly portrayed in *Lothair* (1870), when Disraeli was persuaded that nostalgia for Pre-Reformation days would lose votes. Young England,
and the other medievalising movements, were antidotes for the
liberal utilitarianism of the age, a plea for the restoration of
colour and feeling to modern life. "Man is only truly great
when he acts from the passions; never irresistible but when he
appeals to the Imagination," Sidonia tells Coningsby. But a
sweeping reinterpretation of the English past, whose annals the
Whigs were supposed to have mischievously distorted, did not
lessen the anachronism of Young England's proposals in the
present.

England's decadence was thought to have begun with the
dissolution of the monasteries by Henry VIII. Imputations of
corruption were, according to Disraeli, merely the plunderers'
special pleading: the monks were particular friends of the poor,
and in *Coningsby*, the Young Englander, Eustace Lyle, revives
monastic customs with an alms-giving twice a week at St
Genevieve, his modern but richly decorated Gothic mansion.
On the plunder from the monasteries were founded the fortunes
of what became the "factitious aristocracy" of the Whigs, who
aimed at establishing "a high aristocratic republic on the model
of the Venetian", where the Doge was a figurehead, and power
was monopolised by a Great Council of nobles. Exclusion was
the Venetian and Whig principle: the national life was to be
ordered without reference to monarchy, church and people.
Charles I died trying to protect his people from his Parliament,
which resented ship-money as a tax on the rich and chose to
burden the poor with customs and excise. In 1640, the Venetian
Constitution would have triumphed had it not been for the Puritans, but "Geneva beat Venice", and the consummation was de-

30

layed till the next century. James II did not intend to restore Catholicism to England, but he gave that impression, which was an excuse for his expulsion. William III was too great a man to be reduced to a doge, and the struggle was not resolved until the end of Queen Anne's reign. The new dynasty succeeded on Venetian terms, and George I, George II and an unwilling George III were all doges.

The Young Englanders were heirs to Bolingbroke and other tenants of Disraeli's Tory pantheon who, through the dark years, had recalled the blessings of the old free monarchy and endeavoured to keep Venice at bay. But the situation had changed. The Venetian Constitution had passed away with the 1832 Reform Act, which might only seem to augur democracy: "if the peers have ceased to be magnificoes, may it not also happen that the Sovereign may cease to be a Doge?" At last, perhaps, the English system was to be restored. It was not stated whether the Conservative party was to be converted to Young England principles, or whether the founding of a new party would be necessary. Disraeli was inclined to despise Parliament and welcome the nemesis of its past ambition. Institutions representative only in name were dispensable when the printing press could convey public opinion. Any form of government would be decisively influenced in its conduct by the national character, and the nation must be taught to aspire to the good and the great. Consequently, there was no reason why supreme power should not be entrusted to the doge unchained.

Then might be restored the heroic age before the Dissolution, when monarch, church and people exerted their due national influence, and were not hamstrung by secret committees of nobles. The spectre of Benthamism was raised only by the iniquities of the Venetian Constitution, and would be exorcised. The Church would be disestablished, so that the priests of God might resume their role as tribunes of the people. The popular condition had declined sharply since the fifteenth century, when the peasantry ate flesh every day, never drank water, and was decently housed and clothed. But this was more than "a knife and fork question": ancient feudal feeling was not dead and might be revived. England's present "race of serfs, who are called labourers and who burn ricks", must be invested with the ceremony and privilege which had once bred a loyal and animated peasantry.

With sculptured churches, Norman Yoke and a distaste for Erastianism, *Sybil* blends the prevailing strains of medievalism. Bitter observations on the artisan's supplanting by the capitalist's new slave, the machine with its passive attendant, anticipate Ruskin's thesis in "The Nature of Gothic". We are reminded, too, of Pugin's contrasting plates of the same town in 1440 and 1840. The nineteenth-century built workhouses instead of monasteries, and the population of Marney "took refuge in conventicles" against a vicar whose two sermons a week urged humility and gratitude for earthly blessings. But Disraeli was not a conscious eclectic, and despite the similarities with *Past and Present*, we do not know that he ever read Carlyle. The various expressions of nostalgia for the Middle Ages were the premature lament of a class for its heyday in the past.

Disraeli's version of the Norman Yoke in *Sybil* was as idiosyncratic as Bulwer's in *Harold* (1848), or Charles Kingsley's in *Hereward the Wake* (1865). The heroine, whose favourite reading is entitled "The History of the Conquest of England by the Normans", wishes that the battle of Hastings were to be fought over again, and that she might have a hand in it. England in the nineteenth century was still divided between the conquerors, a pseudo-Norman nobility as mean as the original Normans were barbarous, and the conquered people, descendants of the Saxons. "The spirit of Conquest has adapted itself to the changing circumstances of ages, and however its results vary in form, in degree they are much the same." But the best aristocratic veins tempered Norman with Saxon blood, and a fresh infusion is heralded by the revelation of the people's Sybil as a disguised aristocrat. The dissolution of the monasteries, whose plunder established the fortunes of the Venetian aristocracy, "was worse than the Norman conquest". Queen Victoria, already endowed with Saxon blood and beauty, succeeds to her throne after the wreck of the Venetian Constitution by the Reform Act, and must "break the last links in the chain of Saxon thraldom" by refusing to be a Doge and releasing her subjects from the oppression of the pseudo-Norman Venetians.

Disraeli confined the extravagances of the Young England

creed to his novels, and in *Coningsby* and *Sybil,* he did not try very earnestly to systematise his prescriptions or show how they might be realised. In 1847, Monkton Milnes remarked of *Sybil* that the "two nations" quandary was not resolved by the marriage of two persons, both of whom were rich rather than poor. Interests of reinvigorated Saxon aristocracy and Saxon masses were too readily identified, and the conflict between rich and poor ceded to one between Saxons and others. Then the solution was to expel the degenerates: the pseudo-Norman Venetians; the middle-class millowners, Shuffle and Screw (the good capitalist, Trafford, has "gentle blood in his veins"), whose exclusive withdrawal from their dependants echoed that of their unholy allies; and the repulsive and tyrannical Hatton, the workman disputing with the aristocracy its function of guiding the masses. Wishing to rouse his contemporaries, Disraeli did not despise wilful eccentricity. His bizarre doctrines had less obvious impact than his ringlets and canary-coloured waistcoats, and Young England remained the cult of a few individuals. But the ideas did not die away, and gained fresh currency in the 1880s.

* * *

A. W. N. Pugin was the first man with a serious understanding of Gothic architecture, and he was serious too in anticipating its imminent revival. He established the important principle that any revival depended on "a restoration of the ancient feelings and sentiments" which the architecture originally expressed: Kenneth Clark notes in *The Gothic Revival* that so far as he is aware, the idea of style as organically connected with society is not to be found in eighteenth-century writings. The feelings and sentiments to which Pugin referred were those of medieval Catholicism, so that the revival of Gothic architecture was conditional on England's returning to Rome. "Men must learn that the period hitherto called dark and ignorant far excelled our own age in wisdom, that art ceased when it is said to have revived, that superstition was piety, and bigotry faith," wrote Pugin, sniping at the Enlightenment historians. He was himself a convert to Catholicism, and in the 1830s and 1840s, there was no doubting the revival of Catholicism in England; hence the abuse meted out by such

staunch Protestants as Ainsworth and Charles Kingsley. But that it
was Catholic was not the only truth about medieval civilisation,
and the causes of the rise and decline of the Gothic era were more
complex than Pugin was ready to admit. While generally he
wished to show that his own century was very unlike the Middle
Ages, he was reduced to claiming that both periods were governed
by roughly the same laws and political economy.

More typically, in Pugin's first book *Contrasts* (1836), the
Middle Ages were distinguished by their unity of faith, and the
universal belief that all men were equal in the sight of God. The
"Catholic town in 1440" is composed almost entirely of churches.
In the companion portrait of the same town in 1840, there are
still places of worship amidst the gas works, lunatic asylum and
jail, but religious harmony has succumbed to the dissidence of
competing sects. There are Baptists, Unitarians, Wesleyans, New
Christians and Quakers, while Mr Evans has a chapel to himself,
and St Botolph's has been replaced by the Socialist Hall of
Science. In 1840, the destitute live in workhouses, not alms-
houses. Another etching shows a medieval citizen drinking freely
from a Gothic conduit, while the modern pump is padlocked,
and an urchin is being turned away.

In the 1840s, Ruskin mocked the Gothic Revival, but in
1853, at the end of the third volume of *The Stones of Venice*,
he wrote that the Gothic style must be adapted in England. Pugin
had thought that the essence of Gothic was its Catholic spirit,
and that the Catholic resurgence in England heralded a return to
the architecture of the Middle Ages. Ruskin, on the other hand,
argued that Gothic expressed human impulses without relation
to the Roman Church, but not stultified in the Middle Ages: a
revival depended on transforming the social values of his own
age, obsessed with the profit motive. His regard for the old
Gothic did not make him an orthodox revivalist, and he had to
persuade the movement of the futility of copying medieval designs.

In *The Stones of Venice*, Ruskin dated Venetian Gothic from
1301, when the Ducal Palace began to be built, to 1424, the
year of its demolition. "That hammer stroke," he wrote, "was the
first act of the period properly called the 'Renaissance'. It was
the knell of the architecture of Venice—and of Venice itself."
Pugin's concern with the relationship between religion and archi-

tecture was extended to show how the arts reflected states of society, and Ruskin condemned Renaissance architecture in so far as it was informed by values which were corrupt. The abundance and diversity of Gothic ornament, he claimed, allowed the less skilled artisans to experiment and create within the bounds set by a paternal guidance: blunders were inevitable, but only when the workman thought for himself was he revealed in the full majesty of his humanity. The fall from Eden was more fortunate than the fall from Gothic.

The third volume of *The Stones of Venice* was entitled "The Fall". Renaissance architecture expressed "aristocracy in its worst characters; coldness, perfectness of training, incapability of emotion, want of sympathy with the weaknesses of lower men, haughty self-sufficiency". The execution of ornament, where "the inferior detail becomes principle", required skill and knowledge as great as the designer's. Too high standards were demanded of the workman: pursuit of perfect finish turned him into a mechanical slave. The crux of Ruskin's argument was that the division of labour between lordly designer and the hireling who worked to his specifications was still the bane of nineteenth-century England. "The carvers and painters are our servants— quite subordinate people. They ought to be glad if we leave room for them," he bitterly remarked in his preface to *The Two Paths* of 1859. Indeed, England had refined on the worst that the Renaissance could do. Ever more perfect finish was exacted from workers degraded by the monotony of their labour, who might spend their lives polishing the heads of pins or making glass beads. Neither teaching nor preaching would help. Only a general understanding of what kinds of work were humanly satisfying would avoid revolution.

Gothic's great virtue was supposed to be its adaptability: the style had no uniquely ecclesiastical connotations, Ruskin stressed, and that Gothic churches but not Gothic counting-houses should be built showed how English businessmen dissociated their religion from their daily lives. Ruskin succeeded in secularising the Gothic Revival, but was not impressed with the response to his eloquence: "I have had indirect influence on nearly every cheap villa-builder between this and Bromley," he wrote from Denmark Hill in 1872. The medieval architect had expressed in the most appropriate materials social values with which he identified. By 1836, when Pugin was the first to appreciate the principles of Gothic architecture, innovators were using cast-iron columns and plate-glass. That was enough to rule out a contemporary adaptation of Gothic, even granted a revolution in values. Like Pugin, but with a different emphasis, Ruskin hoped for the future because, at heart, England was still a Christian country. "I believe that in a few years more we shall awake from all these errors in astonishment, as from evil dreams; having been preserved, in the midst of their madness, by those hidden roots of active and earnest Christianity which God's grace has bound in the English nation with rods of iron and brass." Here Ruskin was distanced from the moving forces of his age, and his proposals for reform, like the suggestion that guilds instead of capitalists should supervise standards and conditions of work, were abstract and archaic.

Ruskin's history of Venice related marginally to a social and economic structure which, like that of his own age, was always evolving. But Ruskin knew perfectly well that the medieval era was no Shangri-La possible or even desirable to restore: he differed from the orthodox revivalists, who imagined that Gothic had been built on a system of rules, which could be learnt, rather than from sentiments and feelings, which could not. Great art, Ruskin insisted, never repeated itself, but said new and different things, and in 1859, Tennyson was criticised for wasting his powers on *Idylls of the King*, when the poet's charge was to express "the living present". Ruskin wrote of *Past and Present* that it had become a part of himself; his economic analysis was more penetrating than Carlyle's, but distrust of working-class initiatives induced hope for a regeneration of the other classes which was not forthcoming. Having "seen faces, and heard voices, by road and street side, which claimed or conferred as much as ever the loveliest or saddest of Camelot", Ruskin was verging on Camelot when he became Master of the Guild of St George in 1871.

1

The Historical Novel after Scott

The Historical Novel in the 1830s and 1840s

In 1862, the *Saturday Review* commented that the younger
generation's indifference to the Waverley novels showed the increased mental depth and breadth of the age. Condescension towards Scott reflected changing attitudes to the past: there were
discerning critics among the early enthusiasts, and the author of
Waverley was notably complimented by Macaulay and Carlyle.
In an 1828 essay, "History", the young Macaulay scolded historians for recording battles, sieges and ministerial changes, while
neglecting the history of the people:

> Sir Walter Scott . . . has used those fragments of truth which his-
> torians have scornfully thrown behind them in a manner which may
> well excite their envy. He has reconstructed out of their gleanings
> works which, even considered as histories, are scarcely less valuable
> than theirs. But a truly great historian would reclaim those
> materials which the novelist has appropriated. The history of the
> government, and the history of the people, would be exhibited in
> that mode in which alone they can be exhibited justly, in insepar-
> able conjunction and intermixture. We should not then have to look
> for the wars and votes of the Puritans in Clarendon, and for their
> phraseology in Old Mortality; for one half of King James in Hume,
> and for the other half in The Fortunes of Nigel.

There were lessons to be learnt from Scott's concern with popular
life and, more radically, from how that life was conveyed. The
historian, too, should be an artist, could not escape being an
artist, for better or worse. "Facts," Macaulay remarked, "are the
mere dross of history. It is from the abstract truth which inter-

penetrates them, and lies latent among them like gold in the ore, that the mass derives its whole value. . . ." Addressed to historians, Macaulay's words might have been pondered by Bulwer and his imitators, whose serious pretensions as historical novelists were founded on the narrowness of their research.

Victorian historians, and novelists who began to convey the crises of their own time in historical perspective, responded to Scott's genius, but there is no "school of Scott" in historical fiction. Clearly, he was the inspiration for novels dealing with the prehistory of the Victorian present: Charlotte Brontë's *Shirley* (1849), on the Luddites, or Eliot's *Felix Holt* and *Middlemarch* (1871–72), on the period of the First Reform Act. Even in *Shirley*, however, and certainly in Eliot's work, the popular life of the past is caricatured to point a conservative moral. Only Gaskell's *Sylvia's Lovers*, set in the 1790s, treats the recent English past as acutely as *Waverley* treats the Scottish.

The "historical romance" industry which Scott inspired owed nothing to his finest work. There were, though, two Scotts, and the lesser Scott was easier to imitate. This was the writer producing many novels which were little more than potboilers: the *Talismans* and the *Quentin Durwards*. In the novels set outside Scotland, or dealing with a remote past, or both, a nineteenth-century drama is enacted in period costume. This style was adopted by Scott's early disciples, and historical romance dominated a large market for fiction. It is hard to understand the enthusiasm for the dry pastiches of Harrison Ainsworth and G. P. R. James, but in days before the novel was respectable, historical novelists gained from their pretensions towards instruction. "History is but a tiresome thing in itself; it becomes more agreeable the more romance is mixed up with it," says Lady Clarinda in Peacock's *Crotchet Castle* (1831). Critics who censured the romance as a positive evil included among their complaints that everyone's idea of Richard I derived from *Ivanhoe* and *The Talisman*. The romances of Ainsworth, James and the rest had a more integral attraction, however, and in the 1830s and 1840s when these novelists flourished, there was a demand for the kind of escapism which they provided. A dreamy, romanticised past was an antidote for the Chartist-ridden present; while the notion that, through manifold changes of costume,

38

characters remarkably like middle-class Victorians had dominated events, must have instilled confidence to face modern convulsions.

The late 1840s saw the end of the romance's saturation of the market, with Bulwer, infallible index of public taste, publishing his last romance, *Harold*, in 1848. But critical patience was tried for another twenty years; and in 1846, G. H. Lewes in the *Westminster Review* felt that severity was appropriate. "To judge from the number yearly published," wrote Lewes, "one may presume that there is a great demand for historical romance; and to judge from the quality of those published, one may suppose the readers very good-natured, or very ignorant, or both." Since most novels were mediocre, and romances were most of the novels, it followed that the historical romance attracted mediocrity. To produce a passable romance, the novelist needed merely to study Scott and his followers, "to 'cram' for the necessary information about costumes, antiquated forms of speech, and the leading political events of the epoch chosen; and to add thereto the art, so easily learned, of complicating a plot with adventures, imprisonments, and escapes". Lewes distinguished between two species of historical novelist; the one with a superficial knowledge of his period gained from popular histories, and the "crammer", teaching the reader today what he himself learnt yesterday. Here Lewes was probably thinking of Bulwer, despite his warning against cramming in the preface to *The Last Days of Pompeii* (1834). No paraded scholarship, commented Lewes, might substitute for that mastery of the subject which only long familiarity with the chosen period supplied.

Such mastery was Scott's, and Lewes appears, like Macaulay, clearly to recognise the novelist's achievement. "If, for his purposes, he disarranged the order of events a little; no grave historian ever succeeded better in *painting the character of an epoch*." But Lewes shows a profound inability to grasp the nature of Scott's triumph, and his homage is compatible with a theory of the historical novel which is typically mid-Victorian. Historical fiction, it is contended, has more to do than paint the character of an epoch: there is an abstract "moral truth" which the novel is bound to convey, and the moral truth must be modern. Figures presented for our admiration "must have the greatness which we in our day, reverence; and for this any amount of historical anachronism is admissible". The relevance of these remarks to the portrayal of the modern Romola in Renaissance Florence suggests that the praise of the author of *Waverley* is a formality.

The old historical romance, near extinction by the late 1840s, gained a respite when it became a vehicle of propaganda in the 1850s. Charles Kingsley, Wiseman and Newman all used the historical romance as a medium through which to debate the Oxford Movement and the Catholicism to which it seemed to be leading; and perhaps gave the hint to novelists of the 1860s that the romance might also serve for social and political fables. The romances of James and Ainsworth were frankly intended as commercial entertainments. James stayed at Abbotsford, and his early work was praised and encouraged by Scott. Thackeray, who lampooned James in *Barbazure*, still referred to him affectionately as "the veteran, from whose flowing pen we had the books which delighted our younger days, *Darnley*, and *Richelieu*, and *De L'Orme*". More flatteringly, Landor rated James with Scott, and Ainsworth thought that he might well be the author of *Jane Eyre*. James produced as many as fifty-seven romances in the thirty years of his writing career (1829–59), though the critics did not take him seriously in his lifetime, and his popular reputation died with him.

The formula for his romances was an intricate and fast-moving plot, and plenty of pageantry and costume. Generally, the romances were endowed with two titles, one indicating the historical setting and the other the centre of interest; for instance, *The Jacquerie: or, The Lady and the Page* (1841). Both lady and page are very contemporary. "It is by no means my purpose to enter here into the well-known historical details of the period," writes James in *Henry Masterton, of the Adventures of a Young Cavalier* (1832), and he means every word. Notably, however, James feels more free to respond to history when dealing with social turbulence abroad, than in his novel of the English Civil War. "The vices of the higher class of the Parisian people, their intemperance, their debauchery, their infidelity, their contemptible frivolity, were all indulged, enacted, and displayed under the very same roofs where dwelt misery, penury, and labour—and yet they wondered that there came a revolution!", James writes in *Castelneau, or The Ancient Regime* (1841). This is no more than an aside to the reader and bears small relation to the plot, but the period setting occasionally rears its head as it never does in *Henry Masterton*, and the eternal romance of the human heart has the show of competition. Similarly, in *The Jacquerie*, though the novel is on the theme of its subtitle, there is an animus towards demagogues. In his Enlightenment way, with history running through the same patterns interminably, James is mildly interested in the Jacquerie as well as the Lady. He treats the revolutionary era in England too gingerly even to derive a modern polemic.

James was linked, in critical condemnation, with his fellow romancer, Harrison Ainsworth, who in 1834 found fame with his first novel, *Rookwood*. Ainsworth tended to construct his stories round historical monuments, and *The Tower of London* (1840) is one of the few novels equipped with an index. Like Bulwer's *The Last Days of Pompeii*, Ainsworth's *The Tower of London* and *Windsor Castle* (1843) are incongruous mergings of historical romance and guide-book. Lady Jane Grey is lost in admiration before the White Tower, and the reader is informed of repairs and alterations since Lady Jane's time. Throughout, her own history is palpably interrupted by that of the Tower, as well as by buffoonery and descriptions of costume. Like Bulwer and Charles Kingsley, Ainsworth is patriotic and anti-Catholic, with a weakness for moralising. His reduction of the past to nostalgic blocks of stone left contemporary society high and dry, an indisputable reality; and Dickens' apparently Philistine parody of "The Wisdom of our Ancestors" was more a warning against sentimentality in the conservative cause than a mark of his own complacency.

Bulwer's historical romances were more seriously intended than those of James and Ainsworth. *The Last Days of Pompeii* was Bulwer's last romance in the old style. It was embellished with a preface in which he announced his determination to raise "scholarship to the creative", rather than bow creativity to scholarship, to avoid cramming since "nothing can give to a writer a more stiff and uneasy gait than the sudden and hasty adoption of the toga", and altogether to make his characters live and move before the readers' eyes. As usually with Bulwer, the preface is more impressive than the novel, and despite his spurning of mere erudition, there is plenty in evidence: concentration on minute details of dress, a learned discussion of the origins of backgammon, and a guided tour around the Neapolitan museum. The romancer's motives are still impure, and finally Bulwer decides that the fifth century is beyond redemption and will never live and move again. He ends the novel with a despairing appeal to the human heart which he assumed to beat the same under Grecian tunic and Roman toga. "The magician's gift, that revives the dead—that animates the dust of forgotten graves, is not in the author's skill—it is in the heart of the reader!" Sensibly, Bulwer abandoned ancient Greece and Rome, and restricted himself to the last millenium. He took real pride in *Rienzi* (1835), based on the career of the fourteenth-century Italian, and the two novels on English medieval history, *The Last of the Barons* (1843) and *Harold* (1848).

In these works, Bulwer aimed at historical accuracy, which meant fidelity to the facts. Despite the dedication of *Eugene Aram* (1832), and fulsome tributes in prefaces, he disparaged Scott in private, and in a letter of 1827 referred to him as "the Arch Quack of tale-writing to whom I pray night and morning that I may see justice done before I die". Bulwer states in 1853, in the preface to the third edition of *Harold*, that

> there are two ways of employing the materials of History in the service of Romance: the one consists in lending to ideal personages, and to an imaginary fable, the additional interest to be derived from historical groupings: the other, in extracting the main interest of romantic narrative from History itself. Those who adopt the former mode are at liberty to exclude all that does not contribute to theatrical effect or picturesque composition; their fidelity to the period they select is towards the manner and costume, not towards the precise order of events, the moral causes from which the events proceeded, and the physical agencies by which they were influenced and controlled.

Such, according to Bulwer, was the method of Scott, whose concern with the popular life of the past is reduced to an obsession with manners and costume, and abstracted from the moral causes producing the great events. The author of *Ivanhoe*, wrote Bulwer, "employed History to aid Romance". He had a point about that particular novel, but it is significant that *Ivanhoe* should be considered representative Scott. We cannot take seriously Bulwer's self-deprecation, when he records how he contented himself with "the humbler task to employ Romance in the aid of History".

The humbler task was the one prescribed by critical opinion. In the 1830s and 1840s, Ainsworth and James were not derided in comparison with Scott, but blamed for getting facts and dates wrong, sins of which Scott was also convicted. Professional historians were only beginning to show that they could rival the romancers in popular appeal: Carlyle's *French Revolution* was published in 1837, while the first two volumes of Macaulay's *History of England* did not appear until 1849. The romance substituted for more formal instruction, and was bound not to betray the trust of its readers. From the urging of factual accuracy on the romance derived that crossbreed between history and fiction which Bulwer initiated in 1835 with *Rienzi*, and whose prefaces, footnotes and appendices loomed nearly as large as the text.

J. C. Simmons has remarked that Bulwer's prestige as an historian betrayed a disorientation in the historiographical theory of the time. As he intended, Bulwer's novels were reviewed as history rather than fiction, and as late as 1868, E. A. Freeman alluded flatteringly to *Harold* in the second volume of his *History of the Norman Conquest*. In 1867, John Morley asked in the *Fortnightly Review* why

> the attempt to raise history from being a loose parcel of desultory treatises and narratives to the level of a systematic study of connected phenomena, to convert it from a mass of uninterpreted facts into a symmetrical body of instructive generalisations, should excite such resolute antipathy in the minds of some of the most accomplished writers of the day.

Bulwer's novels are full of conflicting notions—the man of the age shall triumph, the virtuous man shall triumph—but readers of the accredited historians were used to such confusion. It did not worry Carlyle that his various explanations of the French Revolution contradicted one another, and the more rigorous procedure of Comtean "scientific" history was thought subversive. Froude could not reconcile Henry Buckle's statistical approach to social phenomena, in his *History of Civilization in England* (1857–61), with God-given free will. The Regius Professor of History at Cambridge in the 1860s was no less than Charles Kingsley. "The real culprit," remarked the *Saturday Review* acidly, "is not Mr Kingsley, but those who put a man in an historical chair who lacks every qualification of an historian." Historians were taken to task for too eagerly following Macaulay's instructions to borrow the art of the novelist, while ignoring the rider that this did not preclude strict documentation; and Macauly himself was considered the most notable romancer. Bulwer's research was too shallow for him reasonably to hope to make a contribution as an historian, but his many appendices gave the impression that here was scholarship, and amidst the prevailing anarchy of historians writing like novelists and novelists like historians, his scholarly reputation survived briefly.

Bulwer's was a sturdily old-fashioned Enlightenment approach, and his new interpretation of the career of Rienzi, last of the Roman tribunes, was founded on his familiarity with human nature: "revenge and patriotism, united in one man of genius and ambition—such are the Archimedian levers that find in fanaticism, the spot out of the world by which to move the world". The impulse towards direct inspection and embodiment derived from Scott was converted into an obsession with factual detail; and so long as the detail was accurately recorded, Bulwer thought the past an open book, since while costume and scenery changed, human nature and the political dilemmas with which it was faced did not. This meant that although Bulwer was vitally concerned with Rienzi, and believed that future historians of the last tribune's tragedy would not ignore his novel with impunity, he could comment on contemporary issues while writing on the past. Almost as much as Disraeli's *Coningsby* and *Sybil*, Bulwer's *Harold* and *The Last of the Barons*, in which Warwick the Kingmaker advocates Young England policies, were about the condition of England in the 1840s.

The works of Disraeli and Bulwer share a proneness to capital letters and ornamental rhetoric, and the novelists were close friends until Disraeli's marriage in 1839: Mary Anne, an intimate of Rosina Bulwer, had slandered Rosina's husband and bore him a grudge. Bulwer, remarks Robert Blake, was a man "whose egotism, foppery and affectation were at least equal to Disraeli's own": they were both dandies, both made a cult of the dead

Byron, both frequented the salons of Lady Blessington, shunned by the ladies but respectable enough for the gentlemen. No less than Disraeli, Bulwer abhorred the exclusive Whigs, and entered Parliament among the flamboyant miscellany of independent Radicals in 1831. Two years earlier in *Devereux*, set in the eighteenth century, he had irritated the *Westminster Review* with a favourable portrayal of Bolingbroke, Disraeli's hero and an inveterate Tory combatant of the Venetian Constitution. In *England and the English* of 1833, Bulwer criticised with a precise aristocratic detachment the timid selfishness of the trading middle class, which political agitation alarmed for its credit and which undertook even necessary reforms only as a last expedient. Bitterly hostile to Free Trade, Bulwer eventually broke with the Liberals; he was disgusted by the predominance that the narrow dogmas of the Manchester school had attained within the party. "Those miserable Cobdens! and visionary Peace Dreamers! What fools they are, and these are the men by whom England herself has been half driven to the brink of revolution." Profoundly appealing to Bulwer, as to Disraeli, was the notion of the working masses and country gentry combining to oust the millocracy and factious Whig magnates.

The Last of the Barons, which was Bulwer's most admired historical novel, appeared in 1843, and offers a striking instance of the difficulty with which Scott's followers emulated his example. Though disapproving of Scott's casual regard for historical fact, Bulwer assimilated from the Waverley novels more than he cared to admit, and stated in his preface that the romance should convey historical uniqueness, "the habits, the motives, and the modes of thought, which constitute the true idiosyncrasy of an age". Scott exposed his uncommitted heroes to the currents of popular life. Accordingly, Bulwer begins by dealing not with Warwick the Kingmaker or Edward IV, but with young Master Marmaduke Nevile, "the type of the provincial cadet of the day, hastening Courtwards to seek his fortune". Since, however, Bulwer is incapable of dramatising the life of the age, his hero has no function, and hastening courtwards hastens his extinction. With history made from above, all attention centres on the court, and poor Nevile sinks without trace, "lost amidst the gigantic characters and fervid passions that alone stand forth in history".

Like Charles Kingsley's *Hereward the Wake* (1865), Bulwer's last romance, *Harold,* relies on the myth of the Norman Yoke which was the inspiration of Scott's *Ivanhoe.* Unhistorically, it was alleged that the Saxons lived freely and equally until oppressed by the invading Normans; and later struggles for popular freedom might be read as continuing the Saxon, essentially English, tradition. On the other hand, after 1688, with the overthrow of the last of the Stuart monarchs, whose attempts towards absolutism had emulated those of their Norman predecessors, this freedom might be seen as preserved in the constitution. The myth was easily adapted to defend the post-1688 establishment, and well before Macaulay, Henry Hallam, in his *Constitutional History of England* (1827), had interpreted the Glorious Revolution as a triumph of Liberal rather than Whig principles. Victorian notions of freedom, with resonances of self-help and *laissez-faire,* could be identified with Saxon democracy and made to seem truly English in contrast with any suggested restriction on the Englishman's heritage of doing as one liked. There is a paean to the "English-Saxon character", first realised in Alfred the Great, in Dickens' *A Child's History of England* (1852–54): "in Europe, Asia, Africa, America, the whole world over; in the desert, in the forest, on the sea; scorched by a burning sun, or frozen by ice that never melts; the Saxon blood remains unchanged". In *Harold,* and especially the royal hero, Bulwer, too, is idealising "the pure Saxon character" of his race.

One of the more charming aspects of the myth was that imperialism and *laissez-faire* were imbued with all the romantic nostalgia of a lost cause. Harold is reasonably described in Bulwer's subtitle as "The Last Saxon King", but in *Hereward the Wake,* Kingsley goes so far as to label his hero, "The Last of the English". As usual, Kingsley is hyperbolical, and he continues to regard himself as an Englishman, just as for Bulwer we are all Saxons now. Both novelists wanted reassurance from history, and the invocation of providence and human nature was outshone by a version of the past which was complimentary to the present. After the 1832 Reform Act, and despite Macaulay's late celebration, the heyday of the Whig oligarchy inspired decreasing enthusiasm, and neither novelist relied on 1688 to win the lost cause. For Bulwer, the Normans were themselves honorary Saxons, integrally free souls, "and had those souls been less free, England had not been enslaved in one age, to become free again, God grant, to the end of time!" In *Hereward the Wake*, all was resolved with the succession of the first English king, Henry II (a description of Henry which is Kingsley's own). Neither Bulwer nor Kingsley were anxious that their rationalisations should convince, and they assumed a similar placidity in their readership.

In *Harold*, Bulwer claimed to have sought "less to portray mere manners . . . than to bring forward the great characters, so carelessly dismissed in the long and loose record of centuries". This is typical Bulwer, but *Harold* is one of the last novels focusing on history's great men. The titles alone of the historical novels that followed registered a change. Instead of *Harold*, *Rienzi* and *The Last of the Barons*, we have *Shirley*, *Esmond* and *Romola*, the last certainly dealing with a great man, Savonarola, but not featuring him in the title, and concerned to define the limits of his greatness. Reade's *The Cloister and the Hearth* has for its hero the reluctant priest Gerard, not great himself, and whose son Erasmus (appearing only as an infant) may be great, but not in the accepted sense of the great man as history-maker. Except for *Shirley*, the new perspective of the historical novel is less the mark of a return to Scott's practice than of an ingrained despair of conveying the past, and if great men do not determine history, it is hard to say what does. Still, the strength of the trend may be measured by Bulwer's abandoning the romance after *Harold*, and by its influence on Wilkie Collins' first novel, *Antonina* (1850), about fifth-century Rome and the visitation of the Goths, and in most respects a conventional Bulweresque imitation. Like several young novelists of the time, Collins feels bound to begin with an historical romance, but finds that once is enough.

Antonina is more revealing than entertaining, and Collins is acutely aware of writing within a tradition that has seen better days. That one chapter should be headed "Rome" merits an apology:

> the perusal of the title to this chapter will we fear excite emotions of apprehension, rather than of curiosity, in the breasts of experienced readers. They will doubtless imagine that it is portentous of long rhapsodies of those wonders of antiquity, the description

of which has long since become absolutely nauseous to them by incessant iteration.

But with a beginner's optimism, Collins is bent on revitalising the romance, as he explains in the preface. His predecessors' mistake has been to make their main characters historical personages. Collins' resolution to avoid this error is not, however, based on an intention to treat the popular life of the age, and he has no brief for the Roman mob. Departing from Bulwer's practice, Collins is still acting on the criterion that the romance should compete with the formal history in its fidelity to fact. The centrality of historical characters in the romance necessitated the author's "adding from invention to what was actually known", and so placing his fiction in unfavourable contrast with the historian's truth. Collins aims to make his imaginary figures "the practical exponents of the spirit of the age"; but this means merely that, as with Bulwer, if the novelist is concerned with the theme of an emergent middle class, it will be entrusted to one character to represent that class. The allegory is ill-sustained, since the characters persist in acquiring private traits militating against their historical role.

In *Antonina*, the interest soon concentrates on character aloof from environment, and we are treated to the sublime spectacle of the heroine "passing, resolute and alone, though the streets of a mighty city, overwhelmed by all that is poignant in human anguish and hideous in human crime". The novel's close is in curious contrast with the stern doctrines of the preface. The chastening experience of converting theory to practice persuades Collins that he was dissembling in the first place, and that the last thing which might be expected from the historical romance was history. "We can claim the reader's attention for historical events no more—the march of our little pageant, arrayed for his pleasure, is over." Collins never again tried to charm the reader with history; and that dismissed as mere pageantry, we are left in the company of the sublime heroine, appealing to all ages alike.

Charles Dickens: "Barnaby Rudge" (1841)

In his first historical novel, *Barnaby Rudge*, Dickens eschewed the distant past and dealt instead with the era of the Gordon

Riots of 1780, vital prehistory to him as 1745 was to Scott. The accidental involvement of the passive Barnaby in the Riots is like Waverley's in the Jacobite rebellion, and Dickens was both conscious of Scott's example and anxious to compete.

Certainly, *Barnaby Rudge* was closer to historical actuality than any since the Waverley novels. But Dickens is most effective when working through poetic description, like that of the ancient Maypole Inn, sustained by its ultimately destructive ivy. When, to convey the character of the epoch through a treatment of popular life, he elaborated the analogy between fathers abusing their offspring and the ruling class's negligence of those to whom paternal care was due, the influence was Bulwer's. The father-son conflicts are too stylised, mirroring rather than mediating broader social tensions. With the older generation standing for the old regime, allegories of class rule are enacted by characters who, not surprisingly, lack internal consistency. Dubiously at his hanging, the irreligious Hugh invokes the wrath of God on his enemies, while his evil father Chester, who soliloquises about his complex and improbable motives for villainy, is sometimes an instance of the hollow vessel making the most noise.

Dickens thought revolution an imminent possibility in his own age, and recognised the provocation. But he was so far from welcoming class warfare that, in *Barnaby Rudge*, the Gordon Riots were dissociated from his portrayal of a decadent society, and Barnaby's story warned merely of the ease with which the innocent might be implicated in mob terror. The Riots became emblematic like the characters. There is no evidence for Dickens' belief that Lord George Gordon had a co-ordinated plan of campaign, but to blame revolt on a crazed mastermind was a conventional tactic. Then, however, Dickens wishes to discredit the rioters because their actions do not coincide with his mistaken view of the Riots. He complains that often, in what he supposed anti-Catholic agitation, Protestant houses were stormed, which is intended as damning proof of the irrationality of the rioters. But that the houses of the rich were attacked, irrespective of the inmates' religion, revealed the true nature of the Riots, and might have suggested to Dickens that to isolate Gordon's bigotry as their cause was wide of the mark.

The image of the ruling class as an irresponsible father was too simplistic, and assumed ultimate bonds between ruling class and populace which limited the options of the rebellious. Either they were maddened or, in the last resort, they supported law and order. Joe Willet, who has defied his father, goes to fight the Americans waging their own war of independence, and loses an arm. Mr Willet is guiltily fascinated by the loss: it is associated with that emotional crippling, the price of compliance, with which he has threatened to inflict Joe. But his guilt is personal, and that the former rebel, turned soldier, should be crippled by the nation is recorded without irony. Adolescent mutiny is sometimes seen not as a struggle towards identity, but as a failure to adjust to necessary norms; and Dickens is ruthless about the fantasies of Sim Tappertit, the rebellious apprentice. Joe's revolt is healthy, but only because, unlike Sim, he never confronts the society whose tyrannical ways his father approves.

Charlotte Brontë: "Shirley" (1849)

In 1849, no one could assume that the Chartist threat was vanquished. The campaign for parliamentary reform grew directly from Luddism, but writing on the Luddites in Shirley, Charlotte Brontë was not dealing with the Chartists in antique guise. There is no confusion between the two: her period is resolutely the 1812 which it claims to be. When she treats the Luddites themselves, her perspective is conventionally conservative. But by looking beyond the ameliorative legislation of the 1830s to the time when laissez-faire was a creed to the ruling class, she analyses the circumstances which provoked Luddism.

The Times reviewer of Shirley complained that "the authoress never seems distinctly to have made up her mind what she was to do; whether to describe the habits and manners of Yorkshire with its social aspects . . . or to paint character or to tell a love story". Actually, the love story tells us most about early nine-teenth-century society. Brontë has been complimented on the accuracy with which she delineates the higher orders: Robert Moore as the mill-owner resenting the French war and consequent restrictions on trade, but wanting government intervention to protect his property, and Helstone as the "Church-and-King" Tory parson. But faced with the Luddite menace, Moore is praised as a type: the guardian of property against the turbulent workers. Shut up in Haworth parsonage during Chartist agitation, Brontë had sensed the isolation of her class in the Luddite days, and was prone to be too gentle to the forces of repression. It is the love story that realises the tendencies and implications of the new capitalism: away from the Luddites, Brontë is not afraid to see Moore historically. This means that parts of the novel are much better than others, and *The Times* was right about the confusion in *Shirley*.

The direct presentation of Luddism shows the middle-class novelist on the defensive. William Cobbett wrote of the 1812 Report of the Secret Committee of the House of Commons that what would most puzzle the ministry was the absence of "evidence to prove a *setting on* . . . evidence to prove a *plot*. . . . They can find no *agitators*". The notion that Luddism was a genuinely popular movement was as alien to Brontë as to the ministry, and in *Shirley*, the Luddites are manipulated by self-seeking outsiders of higher station. Luddism is stimulated by demagoguery or religious frenzy, and we may detect some Anglican prejudice in the portrayal of the "joined Methody", Moses Barraclough, whom Moore (and here he speaks for the author) accuses of inciting the people to outrage for his own bad purposes. Moore's attempted assassin turns out to be "a frantic Antinomian in religion, and a mad leveller in politics", and we are to assume that the levelling is only a consequence of the Antinomianism.

For Charlotte Brontë, Luddism is merely reactionary, a gesture in the face of an inevitable progress. The Luddites are animated by a hatred of the machines, and see no further than the machinery. Brontë was mistaken, though hers remained the orthodox view of Luddism for a hundred years after the appearance of *Shirley*. What Luddism was opposing, E. P. Thompson remarks,

> was the "freedom" of the capitalist to destroy the customs of the trade, whether by new machinery, by the factory system or by unrestricted competition, beating-down wages, undercutting his rivals, and undermining standards of craftsmanship.

While the capitalist might regard the advent of machinery as inevitable, and many of the smaller masters encouraged the re-

51

sistance, the working class "could see no natural law by which one man, or a few men, could engage in practices which brought manifest injury to their fellows".

Like Carlyle responding to Chartism, Brontë cannot admit the popular movement's intelligence, but like Carlyle too, and unlike the complacent philosophers of *laissez-faire* whom he criticised, the supposed irrationality of the protest does not cause her to make light of the underlying misery. What saves her treatment of Luddism from mere conventionality is the insight gained by working from her own oppressed position within society. She sees that wealthy males treat both women and workers as pathetically deprived of the full humanity of their masters. William Farren, an "honest" working man opposed to Luddism, is still allowed to remark: "invention may be all right, but I know it isn't right for folks to starve. Them that governs mun find a way to help us; they mun make fresh orderations". This contradicts Brontë's suggestion that the misery of the workers is inevitable, and her finer social sense does not accept the inevitability, though she may need to resort to the notion. That her real attitude is Farren's is indicated by Caroline Helstone's meditation on the plight of the single woman:

> nobody in particular is to blame, that I can see, for the state in which things are; and I cannot tell, however much I puzzle over it, how they are to be altered for the better; but I feel there is something wrong somewhere. I believe single women should have more to do—better chances of interesting and profitable occupation than they possess now.

Profitable occupation is what the Luddites are fighting for, and the inability here to allot blame is not meant to suggest a fatality in the circumstances surrounding the single woman. When later Brontë writes that "old maids, like the houseless and unemployed poor, should not ask for a place and an occupation in the world; the demand disturbs the happy and rich . . .", she explicitly associates the lots of women and workers.

The especial scorn attaching to old maids extends to all women, who are to find fulfilment in assimilation by their husbands. Moore is entangled both with his cousin, Caroline Helstone, whom he ultimately marries, and with Shirley Keeldar, the heiress to whom he proposes so that her fortune shall redeem his precarious finances. Shirley is shocked by such conduct from the hitherto gentlemanly Moore, who absorbs his lesson: "henceforth, credit and commerce must take care of themselves". Moore's relations with Caroline Helstone are also shaped by economic pressures, and by the creed which rids him of responsibility to the starving poor. Caroline regards the sensibility of the man whom she loves as alien and disturbing, and speculates on Moore's

> feelings, on his life, on his fears, on his fate; mused over the mystery of "business", tried to comprehend more about it than had ever been told her – to understand its perplexities, liabilities, duties, exactions; endeavoured to realise the state of mind of a "man of business", to enter into it, feel what he would feel, aspire to what he would aspire.

The business mentality is experienced by Caroline as disruptive of the known patterns of life, very much as it was experienced by the Luddites themselves. Opposed to the riotous workers, Moore stands for courageous common sense as against wild fanaticism, but dealing with the private Moore, Brontë is less certain that common sense is monopolised by the capitalist.

Only so long as personal relations are unresolved can they reflect the social situation, and there can be no equivalent to the happy pairing-off of Shirley and Louis, Robert and Caroline. The intended resonances of Shirley's engaging herself not to Robert Moore, but to his impecunious brother Louis, her former tutor, are still-born. She comforts Louis for his lack of fortune and rank by daring him at his peril to "ever again name such sordid things as money, or poverty, or inequality". Here, private and social themes in *Shirley* have fallen apart: the not-naming is too like the fashion in which the rich and happy in society treat old maids and the poor. Like Gaskell's John Thornton in *North and South* (1854–55), Robert Moore has learnt to be considerate towards his workers: "I have seen the necessity of doing good; I have learnt the downright folly of being selfish". The reactionary Luddites must now adapt to a humanised capitalism. But though Moore tells Caroline that "the houseless, the starving, the unemployed shall come to Hollow's Mill from far and near", his conversion has a limited significance. The divisive force of capitalism, sensed by Caroline Helstone in her relations with Moore and against whose consequences the Luddites fought, can be glossed over merely. An authentic ending would have entailed recognition not only of the alien attitudes to trade which provoked Luddism, but also of the protest's strength and intelligence, which Charlotte Brontë could not allow.

The Historical Novel in the 1850s and 1860s

In *Rienzi*, *The Last of the Barons* and *Harold*, the romance's contemporary preoccupations did not mean that the historical interest was frivolous, since Bulwer believed that the same problems recurred. By the 1850s, it was widely assumed that the real history was private, and that the romance's concern would be with the present. The subtitle to *Hypatia* (1853), "New Foes with an Old Face", conceded that Charles Kingsley was bent on reflecting his own era in the past. Despite his parallels, Bulwer had granted the past an uniqueness which he was unable to convey, and had abandoned such early periods as that of Kingsley's fifth-century Alexandria as beyond embodiment.

While overtly writing on the evils of the Alexandrian church, Kingsley was campaigning against the Tractarians. The past's obscurity was absolute, since even in the present, the observer was reduced to speculation. "In the pettiest character there are unfathomable depths, which the poet, all-seeing though he may pretend to be, can never analyse, but must only dimly guess at, and still more dimly sketch by the actions which they beget." The past can be reconstructed only in external detail and by hard labour, and C. Kegan Paul wrote to Mrs Kingsley how struck he was with the extraordinary pains taken by her husband: "we spent one whole day in searching the four folio volumes of Synesius for a fact he thought was there, and which was found at last". Such was the price of using history for propaganda, all the heavier because the history was felt to be irrelevant. As Kingsley remarked, *Hypatia*'s readers had been shown "their own likenesses in toga and tunic, instead of coat and bonnet".

Westward Ho! (1855), like *Hypatia*, was a tract for the times, though it achieved its aim less by mirroring the present in the past, than by the celebration of that period when the timeless

English virtues were best exemplified. Kingsley wrote as a recruiting agent for the Crimean War, and was intent on impressing his readers with the view that the English fighting in the Crimea were worthy successors to the scourges of the Spanish Main. He especially admires the Elizabethans because they were free from introspection. Their mighty conquests were "achieved with the laughing recklessness of boys at play", and the jingoistic Kingsley is sustaining the tradition.

Thackeray was more serious, and more optimistic, about recreating the past. He was stimulated by Macaulay's essay, "History", where historians were recommended to follow Scott, and by the later example of the *History of England* (1849–61). But the title of *Vanity Fair* (1847–48), set in the era of Waterloo, suggests the author's weariness of a humanity changing only in costume:

> at the time whereof we are writing, though the Great George was on the throne and ladies wore *gigots* and large combs like tortoiseshell shovels in their hair, instead of the simple sleeves and lovely wreaths which are actually in fashion, the manners of the very polite world were not, I take it, essentially different from those of the present day: and their amusements pretty similar.

Such is the ruling tone of the novel, and obviously, Thackeray is delineating 1840s characters in the faith that any anachronism will be inconsequential. On the other hand, he seems bent on pointing the moral that there is no immunity from history. By escaping from Elba, Napoleon brings about a crash on the Stock Exchange, and so Mr Sedley is ruined. Thackeray is unable to resolve the two views.

The "Vanity Fair" disillusion may be explained as an admission of Thackeray's own failure to recapture the past. Macaulay wrote in his essay that

> the upper current of society presents no certain criterion by which we can judge of the direction in which the under-current flows. We read of defeats and victories. But we know that nations may be miserable amidst victories and prosperous amidst defeats.

In *Esmond* (1852), Thackeray follows Macaulay in denouncing the court history of battles and sieges which has "nothing to do with the registering of the affairs of the common people", and it is fitting in *Vanity Fair* that Waterloo should be briefly recorded, and that while the characters are involved in the battle and its issue, most of the novel should be devoted to relating their personal misery or prosperity. Mr Sedley is precisely "miserable amidst victories", and this is the true history, "familiar rather than heroick", as Thackeray described it in *Esmond*. But although like Macaulay, Thackeray wants to follow Scott in shunning court history for a broader analysis of the character of the epoch, he has no substitute for court history. Thackeray does not confine himself to the upper current of society in *Vanity Fair*, but cannot reach beneath the rising middle class, and neglects popular affairs. Once battles and sieges are given only their limited due, we do not find the alternative history advocated by Macaulay, and dealing with the silent revolutions of "the changes of manners and morals, the transition of communities from poverty to wealth". And so, in the absence of any perspective on the past, the Ecclesiastes moralising becomes the prevalent strain in the novel.

Esmond suffers in the same way as *Vanity Fair*. The novel, masquerading as an eighteenth-century memoir, is an attempt to revive that century's social realist tradition. But Thackeray, writing in 1852, has none of Fielding's sensitivity to the popular life of the age, whose economic history is disregarded. Dismissing court history, Thackeray reduces history to accident: instead of great men, "trifles" rule the course of the world, "where a gnat often plays a greater part than an elephant, and a molehill, as we know in King William's case, can upset an empire". This, the Cleopatra's nose fallacy, implies the total subjectivity of historical judgments. The hero, Henry Esmond, is slighted by Marlborough at a levée, and the portrayal of the Duke is consequently unfavourable. The only qualification is that "we have but to change the point of view, and the greatest action looks mean; as we turn the perspective-glass, and a giant appears a pigmy. You may describe, but who can tell whether your sight is clear or not, or your means of information accurate?"

Esmond is one of the few English novels to which Lukacs gives attention in *The Historical Novel*, and he makes the distinction that whereas Thackeray's history is accident determined by trifles, "Scott's Waverley also joins the Stuart rebellion by accident;

but he is simply there as a foil to those for whom the revolt is a social-historical necessity". And Lukacs remarks that by showing Marlborough, Steele and Addison as private individuals, Thackeray fails to locate their historical significance. Embittered by the Vanity Fair of his own age and seeing its vices and hypocrisies anticipated in the preceding century, all Thackeray had to oppose to an alien history was the decency and integrity of his hero. Because decency was overburdened, and also because Thackeray, remote from the eighteenth century, was anxious to avoid anachronism, his hero emerges as a tedious prig. Critics who enthused over *Esmond* granted its failure as an historical novel. "A modern mind shines through the external coat," wrote the *National Review*, and consequently, "it is as a tale we look at it".

Thackeray's serious historical intention links *Esmond* with the novels of Dickens and Eliot which followed; and so, of course, does his estrangement from history. What distinguishes *Esmond* from *A Tale of Two Cities* and *Felix Holt* is Thackeray's consciousness of the estrangement, which is almost the theme of the novel. The point of Esmond's final departure for America is that he as well as Thackeray is retiring from history and the European past. The bewilderment in the face of history, which impressed Thackeray as a new and disturbing sensation, is by Dickens and Eliot assumed as a normative aspect of the human condition. When Romola leaves Florence and plays Madonna in the plague-stricken village, she is as much removed from history as Esmond when he goes to America; but the escapism here is certainly not supposed to be Romola's.

Esmond's inferior successor, *The Virginians*, featuring the grandchildren of Henry Esmond, was serialised from 1857–59, when Dickens was writing *A Tale of Two Cities*. In *The Virginians*, Thackeray placidly denies that "human nature is very much changed in the last hundred years". This kind of remark was a commonplace of Enlightenment history, and reappears with a cynical edge in the work of Dickens and Eliot, but has no parallel in *Esmond*, where Thackeray feels that the uniqueness of the age is there to be conveyed. Problems about perspective which were vexing to Esmond are now related to the human condition: even contemporaries are divided one from another.

I declare we know nothing of anybody (but *that* for my part I know better and better every day). You enter smiling to see your new acquaintance, Mrs A. and her charming family. You make your bow in the elegant drawing room of Mr and Mrs B.? I tell you that in your course through life you are for ever putting your great clumsy foot upon the mute invisible wounds of bleeding tragedies.

Esmond was not so far withdrawn from history as to prevent his eager anticipation of American independence, but it seems reasonable to associate Thackeray's later view with the weary conservatism with which the hero of *The Virginians* ends: "The prize is not always to the brave. In our revolution it certainly did fall, for once and for a wonder, to the most deserving: but who knows his enemies now?"

The Virginians is more of an entertainment in the Ainsworthian manner than a serious historical attempt; though it is significant that the historical novel should descend to entertainment in Thackeray's hands. The novels that followed—Reade's *The Cloister and the Hearth* (1861), Eliot's *Romola*—were gravely intended, but not as historical fiction; though the withdrawal from history is neither a theme (as in *Esmond*), nor a consequence of the novel-writing process. The imaginative excursion into the past too disturbing for Dickens to sustain in *A Tale of Two Cities* is never initiated in these later works, whose subject is the heart beating the same under any costume.

Like Thackeray, Reade begins his novel anxious to debunk that history whose moving agents were "great men", and to concentrate on the common life of the age. The opening paragraphs of *The Cloister and the Hearth* set forth an anti-Carlylian theory of the hero. But again like Thackeray, Reade has no sense of the popular life of the past, and it is more than a failure of embodiment. Scott could not embody medieval life, but he had a perspective on the currents of the age which Reade lacks. His modernised hero and heroine inhabit alien terrain throughout. Late in the novel, Reade admits the modernisation in contrasting Gerard and Margaret, who "were before their age", with "your true medieval. Proud, amorous, vindictive, generous, cunning, impulsive, unprincipled; and ignorant as dirt". Gerard and Margaret are endowed with the Victorian virtues, and one strand of the plot becomes Margaret's typically feminine anxiety to secure her marriage lines. In his antipathy to medievalism, Reade was careful to work from those sources most out of sympathy with their own age, and his version of the past was no more than the Whiggish, anti-Catholic propaganda of the Enlightenment historians. Ironically, as Wayne Burns has remarked, it was also distinctively Carlylian in a novel intended as a defiance of Carlyle, and Gerard is not the unsung hero of common life, but the superman in antagonism to his times.

For both Reade and Eliot, the recapturing of the past meant an amassing of factual detail. Reade, who compiled *The Cloister and the Hearth* with the help of a card-index, feared wearing his mind out, and was riddled with misgivings about the method that he employed: "sometimes I say, it must be dangerous to overload fiction with facts." In *Blackwoods* for November, 1863, Margaret Oliphant associated the meticulousness of recent historical novels with the Pre-Raphaelite movement in painting.

> It is harder work now to write a historical novel than it used to be in the days of Sir Walter, when it cost the romancer no scruple of conscience to put a new saint into the calendar for the sake of a handy oath that would rhyme; and when the great novelist could venture to transport us bodily into the previous centuries, upon his own absolute authority, without citing witnesses, or stopping in the tide of the narrative to prove minutely that he could not be wrong. The pre-Raphaelites have done less good in this branch of art than in that to which they have given their more special attention; for the clearest conviction, that you *ought to see* distinctly what a certain set of accurately-depicted persons were doing in a certain closely-described locality four or five hundred years ago, by no means takes the place of actual sight and presence, such as Scott, with his archaic blunders, had a gift of procuring to his readers. . . .

The Middles Ages were real to Rossetti, who did not feel bound to labour at archaeologically precise detail, but there are similiarities between the working methods of Reade and Eliot, and those of Holman Hunt, who created his period paintings helped by a vast store of eastern props, and had himself to go to the Dead Sea to paint "The Scapegoat".

For many years, painters had ransacked the historical novel for their subjects. In the 1840s, there appeared Elmore's "Rienzi

in the Forum" and Rankley's "Edith finding the Body of Harold",
both from Bulwer; Paul Falconer Poole's "Solomon Eagle exhort-
ing the People to Repentance during the Plague of London" from
Ainsworth's *Old St Paul's* (1841); and William Lindsay Windus'
"Morton before Claverhouse at Tillietudlem" from *Old Mortality*.
But more significant than borrowed themes were the stylistic resemblances. Complaining that Bulwer imparted costume but not
character, the *Saturday Review* remarked that *"Harold* and *The
Last of the Barons* are exactly like Mr Maclise's historical pictures.
They show great power of drawing, but they have no life or
nature". Painters were generally content with the vague "period"
atmosphere permeating G. P. R. James's novels. Before graduating
to his contemporary genre paintings, Frith did several costume
studies, including a series on Dolly Varden from *Barnaby Rudge*.
Dolly looks very Victorian, but her dress is ten years out of date
and modified to lend an eighteenth-century flavour.

The mid-1860s saw the beginnings of the neo-classical revival
associated with the name of Frederic Leighton. Like the novelists,
painters strove for archaeological exactitude, marble floors competing for attention with graceful Romans. Classical subjects
were no novelty in painting, but the statuesque quality of the
work of Leighton and his followers suggested that classical life
was absolutely remote from modern experience. Immersing himself in a legendary and heroic past, Leighton was out of sympathy with those novelists believing that historical characters
were ourselves in toga and tunic. But he illustrated *Romola*,
and the extremes met in disputing the relevance of past to present, either because the past was too different or because it was
essentially the same.

Whether the past was romanticised or assimilated, the result
was to lend to the historical situation in the 1860s an accidental
quality. Contemporary life was also portrayed mechanically,
though modern subjects disallowed the private slants of the artist
that total dominance which they could achieve in the past. For
The Cloister and the Hearth, Reade used the plates in his medieval
source books much as he used the illustrations in newspapers,
when writing on his own age. Wayne Burns remarks that Reade
reproduced "his medieval facts with the same Pre-Raphaelite
fidelity that characterises his exposure of the abuses in Birming-

ham Gaol", and that consequently, "his portrayal of the outward life of the fifteenth century is marvellously full and accurate—in the same way that Frith's paintings, or Kean's stage settings, are marvellously full and accurate". The peculiarity of the genre paintings like Frith's *Derby Day* (1858) is their failure to communicate a sense of corporate life. In meticulous detail, Frith presents gipsy-girls chubby and neatly dressed, and beggars decorously ragged. The carefully posed figures are innocent of interaction or conflict.

Lacking a perspective, Reade was obliged to hunt out and particularise "facts" which were often debatable. The work of Dickens alone is a reminder that such dependency did not characterise novelists writing on contemporary themes in the 1860s. But preparing for *Felix Holt*, George Eliot combed the back files of *The Times* with a thoroughness which did not suggest that she was dealing with an era thirty years previous; and the approach of novelists to the remote past was not merely forced upon them by their subjects. To a degree, it was the only way in which they felt that any period might be conveyed, including their own. In writing his conventionally vituperative novel on trade-unions, *Put Yourself in His Place* (1870), Reade studied Thomas Wright's *Habits and Customs of the Working Classes* (1867), and what he learnt from Wright, his own notes make clear: "intelligent workmen exceptional. 9 out of 10 blackguards and blasphemous. p. 6. Want of courtesy. 7. Drunkenness, outside their trade. Credulity about the bloated Aristocracy". The actual novel is slightly less prejudiced than this would imply, and the union leaders have a certain malicious charm. If Wright had been an historical source about historical unions, one might guess that *Put Yourself in His Place* would have been as forbidding as *The Cloister and the Hearth*.

Reade's *Griffith Gaunt* (1866), with an eighteenth-century setting, bears the same relation to *The Cloister and the Hearth* as *The Virginians* does to *Esmond*. After the mighty and frustrated labour to reconstruct the past, the next "period" novel is more cynical. Only one entry on one notecard indicates that Reade was concerned with historical accuracy; and this is merely an assortment of eighteenth-century idioms and phrases. *Griffith Gaunt* is set in that century because its morals were conveniently loose, and Reade could avoid shocking his audience with the suggestion that Victorians committed bigamy. He had sworn while writing *The Cloister and the Hearth* that "it shall be the last time I ever go out of my age", and sustained his resolution.

Scott's own carelessness over detail caused offence, and the title of a *Saturday Review* article of 1862, "Is Walter Scott a great writer?" was a sign of the times. The answer is still positive, but only because of Scott's warm sympathy and genuine human heart. "History itself was ransacked by him, not for its truth, but for its materials of amusement, and it would be a waste of time to pull to pieces his hasty and fanciful creations under the strong light of modern historical criticism." Bulwer had attacked Scott on similar grounds, but had bathed his criticism in reverence. In the preface to *The Prince and the Page* (1865), Charlotte Yonge lamented that "in these days of exactness even a child's historical romance must point to what the French term its *pieces justificatives*", and had to admit that her own did not lie very deep. *The Dove in the Eagle's Nest* (1866) was for adults, and showed Yonge on her academic mettle, listing her manifold sources on the early Reformation.

By the end of the decade, the romance with scholarly pretensions was dying. In 1858, the *Saturday Review* had thought historical romance "the most ambitious and the most difficult, because the most complete, manner of solving the historical problem". Generally in the 1860s, Scott was denigrated and historical fiction condemned as untrue by reviewers whose criteria were accepted by the novelists. The appearance of histories as entertaining as those by Macaulay and Froude had lessened the demand for sugar-coated pills. The past began to be seen as an adventure playground, and while more romances were published between 1870 and the First World War than in the previous half-century, the great majority were intended for children. In his preface to *Lorna Doone* (1869), R. D. Blackmore was scrupulously modest. His book was subtitled "A Romance of Exmoor", and he explained that he chose the term "romance" through neither daring nor desiring "to claim for it the dignity or cumber it with the difficulty of an historic novel". Critical wrath was neatly evaded, but Blackmore's distinction would not have been acknowledged by Bulwer.

2

The Sensational Calm, 1848–67

The Prelude to Reform

Chartist strength lay outside London, and contrasting with the revolutions abroad, the Chartists' April 10 on Kennington Common might have been designed to persuade the middle class in the metropolis that England was immune from the European disease. Complacency as to the stability of English institutions dates from 1848. 1851, wrote Macaulay, was "long to be remembered as a singularly happy year of peace, plenty, good feeling, innocent pleasure and national glory", but the Exhibition celebrated the class truce of the past three years.

According to contemporary witness, the congratulation was pathetically brief. In an 1862 *Blackwoods* article on "Sensation Novels", whose emergence she related to the spirit of the age, Margaret Oliphant invoked the 1851 'Festival of Peace" only to point a mournful comparison.

> What a wonderful difference in ten years! Instead of linking peaceful hands, and vowing to study war no more, we have turned Industry away from her vaunted work of putting a girdle round the world, and set her to forge thunderbolts in volcanic din and passion. In that momentous interval great wars have begun and ended, and fighting has come into fashion throughout the palpitating earth.

The Crimean War exposed the ruling class's maladministration at home and abroad. Both the Italian Risorgimento and, in 1862, the latest sensation, the American Civil War, raised the spectre of democracy; and English Podsnappery was sorely tried. "The greatest question of our time," wrote *The Times* in 1860, "re-

lates to the influence of the masses on the Government under
which they live. It is a question which is not only English or
American, but affects the whole of Europe." The timidity of
middle-class politicians in foreign affairs, and their overriding
concern for their own security, became in *Essays on Reform*
(1867) an argument for extending the franchise to the workers,
since they alone were capable of exercising a detached moral
judgment on international issues. The middle class, despite the
fashionable sympathy with the Piedmontese cause in Italy (Mazzini was dismissed as a fanatical red republican), was always
ready to subordinate that sympathy to its own putative safety.
R. H. Hutton wrote that anyone remembering the panic which
Napoleon III's Italian expedition, and the prospect of European
war, inspired in 1859 was bound to admit how much Parliament
needed what a fair working-class representation would have
given it: "a certain scorn for the selfishly English point of view,
for the anxious and angry 'What will become of us if this goes
on?' which was echoed about amongst us, while liberty and
national life for the great Italian nation still hung in the bal-
lance".

Struggles abroad were taken as portents (revolution, or civil
war, or both, were regularly anticipated in the press, and Poland,
Italy or America now would be England in ten years' time unless
democracy might be contained), and the manner in which foreign
wars heightened and promoted democratic consciousness in England went some way to substantiate the gloomier prophecies. The
American crisis, and particularly the campaign against threatened
governmental intervention on behalf of the Southern States,
brought together those elements later to combine in the Reform
League, and served as an apprenticeship for the successful reform
agitation of 1866–67. The upper and middle classes, accustomed
to sympathise with oppressed nationalities, affected to regard
the Southern cause in the same light as that of the Poles or
Italians. But what ensured their support was that the South was
in arms against the democracy which, long established in America,
now threatened in England. Lincoln's name was often coupled
with Bright's in denunciation, and the early stages of the Civil
War seemed a direct rebuff for Bright, arch-espouser of the cause
of the North. "Democracy in action has driven one-third of a

great population into open rebellion," commented *The Times* gratefully. From the end of 1862, most aware English workers supported the North, and were determined to resist intervention. Remarking that unionists would have a natural bias towards the North, *The Times* equated not only their politics but their destructive potential, and tortuously insisted that striking miners were bringing the Civil War to England: "precisely the same desolation which has been made so vivid to us by the American contest is inflicted upon hundreds of homes by such a struggle as is now going on in Staffordshire. . . ." The fear that the unions might lead those campaigning for reform in armed struggle in England haunted the middle class at each recession. At the beginning of 1861, *The Times* dolefully regarded "the prospect of several civil wars to come off next summer". England might not look very inflammable, but "fireproof buildings ere this have been reduced to blackened shells, and shaken to their foundations".

Some causes of the prevailing impression in the 1850s and 1860s that the masses shared in the general prosperity are noted by Geoffrey Best: the growth of working-class "respectability", pride in elementary provisions for health, education and housing, and until 1865 the absence of mass democratic movements, persuading the propertied classes that the 'sixties were less hungry than the 'forties. But the optimism was groundless, and Marx was justified in opening his inaugural address of the Working Men's International Association with the declaration: "it is a great fact that the misery of the working masses has not diminished from 1848 to 1864, and yet this period is unrivalled for the development of its industry and the growth of its commerce". The wage-earners did not benefit as a class from the mid-Victorian boom, and by the late 1860s, according to E. J. Hobsbawn, the working-class family was finding it progressively harder to make ends meet. The economic distress of the years 1866–67 has much to do with the vigour of the reform campaign at that time; earlier in the decade, reform had not captured the popular imagination. Geoffrey Best writes that

> whatever rewards life could hold for the more fortunate of the labouring classes, the skilled and semi-skilled labourers (who comprised about three-fifths of the adult male labouring population),

it only held them *in good times*; and there was at all times this permanent residuum beneath, for some of whom life was permanently hungry and brutish, and for others of whom life was, according to the ebb and flow of prosperity, intermittently anxious and deprived.

The press often warned of the ravages of the residuum (a term introduced by Bright in 1866), in an effort to discourage meetings of the comparatively respectable working-class reformers. The meetings themselves were the first cause for alarm, but fear of the residuum was real enough, and was shared by Bright. Householders kept firearms in their homes, and the windows of smart houses were fitted with shutters and bars, while the police's function was as far as possible to guarantee the seclusion of polite neighbourhoods. Carlyle was roused to fury by roughs addressing him in the street, and part of the point of admitting the artisan to the franchise was that thereby one penetrated nearer the social depths, and could better legislate to keep the residuum in order.

The middle class knew something of the actual composition of the residuum. The progress of Mr Sedley in *Vanity Fair* shows Thackeray's awareness of how men might be reduced by misfortune and the hazards of trade, and Mantalini's farcical presentation in *Nicholas Nickleby* (1838–39) was Dickens' way of tempering the horrors. As reform agitation gathered momentum, however, there was a tendency to redefine the residuum as the entire working class. In *Culture and Anarchy* (1869), Matthew Arnold remarked that the Hyde Park rough would, of course, "like his class to rule, as the aristocratic class like their class to rule, and the middle class theirs". Increasingly, through the mid-Victorian period, and especially in the 1860s with the advance of the New Model Unions, the middle class was aware of an ideological challenge to its interests, more disturbing than mere anarchy. The main enemy became the politically conscious reformers, and fear of local disorder in the parks cannot be taken seriously. The clamour over the Hyde Park railings in July 1866 was because their overthrow seemed to betray a deliberate attitude towards property. The railings' collapse marked the opening of the floodgates, and the houses in Park Lane would be next in line.

The dramatic change of stance on the reform question evinced by the press in 1867, the swift decision that mass agitation made it more dangerous to resist the reformers than to accede to their demands, was anticipated more than once through the preceding years. On Christmas Day, 1858, *The Times* asserted that gullible unionists were eminently unqualified for the vote. A few weeks later, Bright had struck out on a countrywide campaign to promote reform, and the issue was much less complex: "when an Eastern traveller is surrounded by a tribe of Arabs imperiously demanding *backsheesh*, he ought to choose between the expense of granting their demands and the risk of refusing". For Podsnappery was substituted nervous allusion to the hurricanes sweeping Europe. The series of abortive reform bills, terminating with Gladstone's in 1866 and prompted by continuing agitation, stirred expectation which was never gratified, and in *The Times*'s view aggravated a parlous situation. For years prior to the concession of 1867, the middle class grappled with the dilemma bleakly resolved by Tocqueville in *Democracy in America*, a masterly analysis moving Victorians all the more for the slanted translation by Henry Reeve, which heightened the terrors of the oncoming democracy:

> when I am told that since the laws are weak and the populace is wild, since passions are excited and the authority of virtue is paralyzed, no measures must be taken to increase the rights of democracy; I reply, that it is for these very reasons that some measures of the kind must be taken. . . .

A hint of sustained unrest converted the middle class to Tocqueville's opinion. The late 1850s saw the rise of the great strike movements, and between 1859 and 1861, the Builders' Union in London struck for a nine-hour day and was supported by the whole labour movement. According to the *Saturday Review*, such revelations of working-class solidarity "thoroughly frightened the middle classes", who linked trade disturbances with the demand for reform as twin portents of democracy. They were right that there was a connection: radical employers backed the reform campaign in the 1850s to deter unionists from assuming that their interests were at odds with those of their masters. Generally, at this time, the militancy of the unions was a reason for resisting reform at all costs. They took no part in the campaign until the autumn of 1866, but when they did, their presence persuaded most of the press to agree with the employers that unionists were less dangerous inside than outside the representative system, and to support the Bill the following year.

"It seems very difficult not to believe in some kind of calm through at least the years 1850–65", writes Geoffrey Best. But the evidence suggests that Margaret Oliphant, who took her readers' concurrence for granted, was not alone in regarding the serenity of 1851 as a fools' paradise. Of course, the demands of the Chartists were more "revolutionary" than those of the New Model Unions in the late 1850s and 1860s when, Royden Harrison remarks, working-class politics "became less of a 'knife and fork' and more of a 'collar and tie' question". But the unions' organisation was something new in the labour movement. Opposing reform, *The Times* thought that extension of the franchise would place the rich in the position of the masters in the building trade, but without even the defence of combination. While it was convenient to assume that any unionist was liable to commit the atrocities of the Sheffield Saw-Grinders and their secretary Broadhead, no doubt that view was widespread, and each crisis was seen as a possible prelude to revolution. Those urging education on the workers were, perhaps, dubiously entitled to do so, and based their forecasts on abstract calculations, the radical John Stuart Mill as much as the conservatives. The peaceful demeanour of the Lancashire workers during the cotton famine, caused by the North's blockade of Southern ports, was taken as a hopeful pointer towards the reconciliation of classes, but an instance of looting checked the middle-class plaudits. The former heroes of the hour were now "on the high road to take rank with the permanent dangerous classes", according to *The Times*, which warned of open insurrection throughout Lancashire and Cheshire.

By 1865, the Fenian risings had begun, and the troubles in Ireland seemed a measure of what might be expected from English workers. American origins were found for the revolt, but more disturbing, Fenianism could not be attributed to demagogues. *The Times* wrote that the movement "was entirely the work of the lower classes, and as such is signalized by many

68

features closely resembling the rebellion of Jack Cade". The cast of mind that paralleled Cade's fifteen-century mob with the Fenians was unlikely to differentiate between Ireland and England in the 1860s, and worst suspicions seemed confirmed when a meeting at St Martin's Hall organised by Edmund Beales, President of the Reform League, manifested its solidarity with the Fenians, and acclaimed the name of Ireland. Warily, the *Saturday Review* commented that "the profound and unanimous expression of feeling, even to the extent of sympathy with rank rebellion, was in itself very remarkable". Trade unions began to be compared to the Fenian congresses in session in New York, and when the Sheffield atrocities came to light in October 1866, ominous resemblances were detected with the Irish agrarian murders. These fears were not altogether imaginary, and Gustave-Paul Cluseret, who was afterwards Chief of Staff of the Paris Commune, was trying to establish a Fenian-Reform League alliance. Suspicion of the association was a main motive of *Blackwoods'* accession to the demands of the reformers, or at least served as such. G. R. Gleig, in March 1867, did not doubt that had the Fenian attack on Chester Castle succeeded, disturbances in St Giles and Islington would have followed, and saw in the state of England, with its weak government, numerous but divided opposition, and the mounting popular pressure out of doors, "precisely such a disposition as has in all times past preceded and worked up to revolution". In May 1867, wrath was aroused by the Positivist petition on behalf of the Fenian prisoners, and the *Saturday Review* compared Beesly and his colleagues with the Girondists of the great French Revolution, "the weakest and not the least mischievous among the revolutionary promoters of the Reign of Terror". In her "Felix Holt's Address" of 1868, George Eliot was still invoking the example of Ireland, and implicitly urging English workers not to emulate the Fenian response to social grievances, "the law of no man's making".

The Reform League demonstration in Hyde Park in July 1866, which excited enthusiasm for reform in the towns, provoked bluster about a possible backlash of the respectability, and Matthew Arnold was struck with "the alarmed conservative feeling" detectable amongst middle-class tradesmen and employers: "their disgust at Bright and the working-class is as deep as that

of the aristocratic world". At this time, Arnold himself was con-
temptuously disapproving of the unions, and in the first edition
of *Culture and Anarchy*, rashly abused the demonstrating workers
in the words of his father: "as for rioting, the old Roman way of
dealing with *that* is always the right one; flog the rank and file,
and fling the ringleaders from the Tarpeian Rock". The issue of
Governor Eyre's bloody suppression of a black revolt in Jamaica,
in October 1865, allowed his supporters to vent their feelings
about the English situation. Bright was on the committee for the
prosecution of the governor: it was the reformers who wished to
bring Eyre to justice, and the ruling class replied by fêting him.
The workers were viewed by Eyre's idolators much as the 13,000
whites in Jamaica, another exposed minority, regarded the
400,000 blacks, and mounting agitation made the governor's
handling of the blacks seem all the more appropriate. Carlyle,
a leading and industrious backer of Eyre, did not mind making
his antidote for popular anarchy a precedent for England, and,
in August 1867 in "Shooting Niagara", counselled patience to
the "chosen of the world", until they could "actually step forth
(sword not yet drawn, but sword ready to be drawn), and say:
'Here are we, Sirs; we also are now minded to *vote*—to all
lengths, as you may perceive' ". To a journalist observer of the
early meetings of the Eyre Defence Committee, "this fiery man
of letters" seemed less merciful than the governor, whose cause
was also espoused by Ruskin, Kingsley, Tennyson and Dickens
(the scientists were more enlightened). In February 1866, Bright
felt that the Tories "could easily excite themselves to serve me
as Gordon has been served in Jamaica", and after the Hyde
Park demonstration in July, Marx remarked that "cur Knox, the
police magistrate of Marylebone, snaps out summary judgment
in a way that shows what would happen if London were Jamaica".
In June 1867, there was a meeting of unionists at Exeter Hall to
denounce the crimes of Broadhead, secretary of the Sheffield Saw-
Grinders, who protected his union against blacklegs by blowing
them up. Engels had noted in 1845 the savagery of the labour
movement in Sheffield: "he who is once a grinder falls into
despair, as though he had sold himself to the devil". When
Beesly turned the tables on middle-class moralists by suggesting

that Broadhead was an amateur in the art of murder compared with Governor Eyre, he nearly lost his chair at London University and was renamed "Professor Beestly" by *Punch*.

At the end of 1865, the *Pall Mall Gazette* had pronounced that the first duty of any reformer was "to show *why* he wants change", and did not doubt that dread of the revolutionary violence of the unenfranchised inspired the reforming zeal of very many M.P.s. That dread was decisive in 1867, and the *Pall Mall* attributed most of the credit to the unions. They were the real principals of the reform struggle, and aimed at nothing less than the dethronement of capital. Perhaps with Marx's I.W.M.A. in mind, the same paper commented how striking it was that while governments wrangled, workers were uniting in fellowship for the advancement of their common interests, a revolution "which though it cause no bloodshed, is not to be made with rose-water". The *Pall Mall*'s overrating of unionist class-consciousness should not obscure its insight into the future of the English labour movement. The limited ambitions of labour leaders in the 1860s were a necessary prelude to the effective militancy of the 1870s and later. For the *Pall Mall*, labour's new sophistication is still a reason for withholding the franchise, but by April 1867, the opposite view, expressed by G. C. Broderick in *Essays on Reform*, was more typical.

It was finally agreed that a large concession was urgent if the reform agitation was not to become a menace, and fear of "revolution by inches", with any yielding on the franchise paving the way to universal suffrage, succumbed to more immediate pressures. "The plain truth is that the bill is what agitation, the competition between two parties violently opposed to each other, and in general the force of circumstances have made it," concluded the *Pall Mall*. Still, a main reason for the 1867 surrender was the widespread conviction that it was probably safe. Walter Bagehot, whose *English Constitution* was serialised in the *Fortnightly Review* just before the demonstrations of 1866–67 shook his belief in deference, thought that the lower classes did not look to politics for change, which was all to the good, since "you can use the best classes" to govern a respectful country. In his introduction to the second edition of 1872, he confessed to being "exceedingly afraid of the ignorant multitude of the new constituencies". But Bagehot's original analysis was nearer the mark than his subsequent misgivings, and the reform agitation did not signify the passing of deference. Engels, who underestimated the final Liberal majority, considered the 1868 election

> a disastrous certificate of poverty for the English proletariat. . . . The *parson* has shown unexpected power and so has the cringing to respectability. Not a single working-class candidate had a ghost of a chance, but my Lord Tumnoddy or any *parvenu* snob could have the workers' vote with pleasure.

The cringing which soured Engels proved Bagehot's point. What made England safe was "deference" and an acceptance of "removable inequalities"; removable, on an individual basis, by steady application of the bourgeois virtues, like sobriety and self-help. Passing the Bill, the ruling classes were relying less on the workers' goodwill than on those "occult and unacknowledged forces which are not dependent upon any legislative machinery", which Leslie Stephen argued to govern society in *Essays on Reform*. Clearly, such forces were already active, as the workers were in a sufficiently massive majority to seize power if they had a mind to. Bright and the middle-class leaders of the Reform League were certainly not questioning the social structure. They saw the problem as privilege, not poverty, and campaigned secure in the faith that their followers were as much attached to self-help, and the other virtues calculated to remove inequalities, as they were themselves. Bright stressed the vote's metaphysical value because he had no legislative programme in mind for the reformed parliament.

Despite its respectable ideology, the Reform League's organised shows of strength assured the passing of the Bill. Confidence that the artisans would respond if their moderation and moral right to the vote were recognised, instead of rebuffed with the scorn of a Robert Lowe, was very different from assuming that the country might escape unscathed if no heed were paid to their importunity. While the League's agitation did not determine the timing of the introduction of the Government Resolutions, it did persuade many backbenchers that reform was urgent and no longer an issue for abstract debate. Members irreconcilably opposed to reform in 1866 gave the Government a confused loyalty in 1867, and Disraeli, furnished with a persuasive argument, could suggest that those who hesitated were imperilling the country. Hodgkinson's amendment, quadrupling the originally proposed extension of the franchise, passed through Parliament with no division and almost no debate. "Had the Members simply closed ranks against the Reform agitation," writes F. B. Smith, considering the argument that League activities only delayed the measure, "they would never have suffered the Bill in its amended form."[1] Royden Harrison suggests the impossibility of divorcing the question of Party calculation and rivalry from the evolution of the labour movement, which "had attained precisely that level of development at which it was safe to concede its enfranchisement and dangerous to withhold it".

The reform agitation of 1866–67 succeeded the composition of those historical novels by Dickens, Eliot, Gaskell and Meredith, with which I am mainly concerned: *Felix Holt* and *Vittoria*, the last of the novels, were published in 1866. But all the novels might be seen as preparations for confronting Hyde Park situations, or worse. The novelists are treating the past to understand the present, and it is a reflection of the mood of the present that their chosen periods are ones of agitation and revolution. Their responses to democracy are as varied as those of the M.P.s who passed the Reform Bill, and Dickens and Eliot are more prone to "the alarmed conservative feeling", whose prevalence Arnold noted following the July demonstration, than Gaskell or Meredith. *A Tale of Two Cities, Romola* and *Felix Holt* are beguiled to a solution impracticable for the worried backbenchers in 1867, and set the world at peace by dissipating popular tumult. *Sylvia's Lovers, Sandra Belloni* and *Vittoria* are also coloured by the fears which Radicals shared with Conservatives; but these novels are sustained attempts to come to terms with democracy through historical analysis. As a group, the historical novels were inspired by the events which induced their subjective tendencies: wars abroad, the growth of the union movement, and the reform agitation, beginning in the late 1850s, that culminated in the Hyde Park demonstrations of 1866 and 1867.

[1] A review of Maurice Cowling's *1867: Disraeli, Gladstone, and Revolution*. *Victorian Studies*, XII (September 1968) pp. 121–22.

The Sensation Novel: The Literature of an Age of Events

Around 1860, the sensation novel supplanted the virtuous "domestic saga" in the esteem of the reading public. Sensation novels and genuine historical novels alike met with antipathy in the reviews. In 1863, H. L. Mansel, who was afterwards professor of ecclesiastical history at Oxford, and dean of St Paul's, branded the sensation novels as "morbid" in their social probing. But *Sylvia's Lovers*, dealing with the 1790s, was also censured as unpleasant reading. Mansel explains the sensation novelist's cult of modernity by the necessity of being "near a mine to be blown up by its explosion": his assumption was called into question when modern explosions were derived from the past.

Two accounts of the sensation novel are worth considering; Mansel's in the *Quarterly*, and Margaret Oliphant's, appearing in *Blackwoods* for May, 1862. The one shows the fear and distrust which the sensation novel inspired in conservative readers, and the other, why that should have been the case. Mansel thought the sensation novel a formative influence on the habits and tastes of his generation, but blamed the new literature for gaining its effects by "preaching to the nerves". These novels, worthless productions according to Mansel (and he included Wilkie Collins' *No Name* in his review of a mass of recent sensation literature), were still indicative of a widespread malaise, and the sensation novel's morbidity was linked with what Mansel termed its didacticism. As soon as a writer conceived a prejudice "against any institution, custom, or fact of the day", his hostility found imaginary embodiment in a sensation novel, and Mansel's list of the institutions (or were they facts?) under attack covered the law and the peerage. For Mansel, this was a game which anyone could play, and he did not attempt to differentiate the novel where authorial prejudice had a local habitation and a name from the one where it lay naked.

Mansel's wholesale rejection of the literary vogue betrayed his own insecurity and that of his class, and his article is remarkable more for that revelation than any intrinsic merit. Margaret Oliphant's, on the other hand, is critically discerning, and interprets the dissidence which Mansel calls morbid. The mood of the

1860s, writes Oliphant, is at odds with the confidence attending and fostered by the Great Exhibition of 1851.

We who once did, and made, and declared ourselves masters of all things, have relapsed into the natural size of humanity before the great events which have given a new character to the age. Though we return with characteristic obstinacy and iteration to the grand display of wealth and skill which in 1851 was a Festival of Peace, we repeat the celebration with very different thoughts. It is a changed world in which we are standing.

The distant roar of European and American wars forms a thrilling accompaniment to the safe life at home. Across the Atlantic,

a race *blasée* and lost in universal *ennui* has bethought itself of the grandest expedient for procuring a new sensation; and albeit we follow at a humble distance, we too begin to feel the need of a supply of new shocks and wonders.

The new sensation literature is a faithful reflection of contemporary currents: it is "natural that art and literature should, in an age which has turned to be one of events, attempt a kindred depth of effect and shock of incident". So far from his morbidly preaching to the nerves, the mark of Wilkie Collins' originality is that, unlike his predecessors in the sensation field (Hawthorne, Bulwer, Dickens), he never overstrains nature. Even Mansel has to admit that the sensation novels are effect as well as cause of a diseased appetite for social anatomy, and Oliphant suggests that a diseased society provoked its own dissection.

As increasingly life was felt to be determined by events beyond human control, values which had expressed generalised aspirations acquired sinister undertones. G. M. Young writes that while the Victorian code of duty and self-restraint still held good, the philosophy on which it was based was breaking up in the 1850s and 1860s, when the fundamental assumptions—that wealth for the few meant eventual welfare for the many, and that the social creed was an authoritative moral guide—were experienced as untenable. Values derived from the *laissez-faire* ethic ceased to seem altogether humane: true morality, perhaps, might be the prerogative of the social rebel. This paradox the sensation novel explored. The name of the hero of *The Woman in White* (1860), Walter Hartright, is an irony, suggesting a harmony of opinion which no longer exists on the constitution of a right heart, and it is ironical, too, that the climax of the novel should be set in that year of fleeting complacency, 1851.

In the novel, Wilkie Collins, asks whether his own generation is not rather too well brought up. Mr Hartright senior's benevolent impulses were one with the social orthodoxy, and his "admirable prudence and self-denial", we are told, left wife and daughter as "independent of the world" after his death as during his lifetime. But by the mid-century, the coinage has been debased. Mrs Catherick is determined to shut her daughter in a respectably private asylum, and Sir Percival Glyde, the sham baronet, reports himself as willing to finance her whim, through his esteem for "honest independence of feeling in any rank of life". The veneer of respectability is worth the trouble of cultivating, and Mrs Catherick, who rehabilitates herself in Welmingham society despite the suspicion of her former affair with Sir Percival, is careful to leave the handsome bible on the coffee table.

The Italian Pesca, ambitious to see his friend Hartright a Member of Parliament, like Sir Percival, is prone to an anglomania only highlighting his incapacity for English artifice. Count Fosco, Sir Percival's friend and mentor, also aspires, but with conscious irony, to respectability. He proves his wife's rectitude by reference to the laws governing domestic relations in England, maliciously taken at its own estimate by the Count as "the land of domestic happiness", and shows that the wife is charged to collude in any depravity in which her husband may engage. As Margaret Oliphant suggests, what is sensational in The Woman in White is the reality underlying the convention. Laura's striving to establish her identity is associated with the "struggle for existence" of the poor in the East End of London, while the social isolation of the ruling class reduces its members to their own states of quarantine. Fosco must impose Order in Italy; the English ruling class can afford to be more discreet, and does not share the Count's exuberance.

Laura's uncle and guardian, Mr Fairlie, is a bedridden invalid inflicted only with "nerves" (Collins argues against Dean Mansel that the nervous malady of the monied classes preceded their novel-reading). Fairlie is both irresponsible and class-conscious, and during what the solicitor Gilmore wishes to be a private

76

interview, grudges dismissing the manservant, supporting some etchings and hence "simply a portfolio stand". The drawing-master, Walter Hartright, we are told, has been treated in the houses of the rich "as a harmless domestic animal". Gilmore is presented to us, through Hartright's eyes, as benignly satisfied with the rewards of a long career; but his Tory orthodoxy is not enough to save him. The solicitor is seized with what seems to be an apoplectic fit, having long complained of "fulness and oppression in the head". Overwork is blamed, but overwork (a prevalent Victorian health-hazard) usually had nervous causes. It is likely, the novel suggests, that Gilmore's collapse derives from the conflict between a benevolent heart and the exactions of the legal profession.

Oppression in the head is endemic in London, where Gilmore works, and Hartright fears gradual suffocation in his chambers at Clement's Inn. He first sees Anne Catherick, the victimised woman in white, in appropriate pose with "her hand pointing to the dark cloud over London". Collins' condemnation of the city owes nothing to jaded romanticism, and indeed, at one point in the novel, he sternly dissociates himself from the pastoral mode: "we go to Nature for comfort in trouble, and sympathy in joy, only in books". In *The Woman in White*, London's evil is specific.

Having rescued Laura from the asylum and intent on evading pursuit, Hartright and Marian make for London and the anonymity which it promises; finally settling, as Hartright relates, in the far East of the city:

> I chose it in a poor and a populous neighbourhood—because the harder the struggle for existence among the men and women about us, the less the risk of their having the time or taking the pains to notice chance strangers who came among them.

The impression of the monied classes is that they are "miserable Spies", as Laura correctly terms Fosco, much to his wrath. In England as well as Italy, the forces of order emulate the conspiratorial network of the revolutionaries; hence the prospect of suffocation which Hartright associates with repellent London. Here, the guerilla techniques which Hartright has acquired in the American jungle are bizarrely apt. Before entering the lodgings shared with Laura and Marian, he walks round by a lonely street, repeatedly glancing back to see if he is followed:

> I had first learnt to use this stratagem against suspected treachery in the wilds of Central America—and now I was practising it again, with the same purpose and with even greater caution, in the heart of civilized London!

The implication is that if, in mid-Victorian London, you think that you are hunted and spied upon, you are not paranoid: you are probably right. The continuing experience of Hartright, Laura and Marian substantiates the intuitions of Anne Catherick, who feels that without rank or title, Hartright can be trusted. Gradually, he understands her, and his cause becomes Anne's and also that of the poor in the East End, as he struggles with Rank and Power, "armed deceit and fortified Success". The sensation which overtakes Hartright on the road to London, inverting his habitual sense of the world—

> it was like a dream. Was I Walter Hartright? was this the well-known, uneventful road, where holiday people strolled on Sundays? Had I really left, little more than an hour since, the quiet, decent, conventionally-domestic atmosphere of my mother's cottage?

—turns out to be the reality, not the dream, pointing Hartright in the right direction, as Anne points to the dark cloud over London.

Anne is the social victim who cannot be reduced to a statistic ("things of this sort happen constantly in my experience. Anonymous letters—unfortunate women—sad state of society," the solicitor Gilmore remarks of Anne's warning letter to Laura). Simply by being personalised, Anne's plight exposes the shallowness of conventional opinion, and she afflicts Hartright with the "vague sense of something like self-reproach". May misfortune always be deemed a punishment for sin, as working-class poverty is held to derive from lavish spending on drink? Not in Anne's case, though she must battle with the customary prejudices. Finally, Hartright throws over the self-help ethic with which he has been instilled, and finds the courage to help Anne instead.

Like Charlotte Brontë in *Shirley*, Wilkie Collins suggests parallels between class oppression and the oppression of women. The predicament of Laura, destined to a marriage which neither attracts nor repels her, is typical, and gradually merges with Anne's. Originally, the women's resemblance is slight, but Laura's beauty is not innately feminine, and depends on a comfortable existence. As her life grows more irksome, the half-sisters become almost identical. Marian Halcombe belies Hartright's presentiment of ideal womanhood (Laura, delicate and listless, is much nearer the mark), when she faces round and reveals a swarthy complexion and a moustache. She lives up to her moustache though, appropriately, it is the foreigner Fosco's adoration that her masculine resource and daring excite.

The eruption of the Italian Risorgimento into the novel (Fosco is a government spy, Pesca a revolutionary agent) is integral, rather than a mechanism for contriving Fosco's destruction. That the champion of order and aristocratic privilege in Italy should also be a criminal would not have surprised Collins' readers, but Fosco's thesis that society acts as the criminal's accomplice extends to England. According to conventional assumption, England was the rock of civil liberties, the thorn in the flesh of foreign despotism. But Pesca can combine adulation for the England of bourgeois myth with a resounding defence of the Italian right to disregard the law and win freedom, and while Pesca is consistently anglophile, the novel is far from implying that the liberty sought by the Italians has conquered in England. On the contrary, the plight of the downtrodden is juxtaposed with the law's remedial impotence. As we cannot blame the Italians for moving outside the law, so we are forbidden to blame Walter Hartright.

There were over a hundred lawyers in the Commons in the 1860s, and not surprisingly, they were slow to reform themselves. Wilkie Collins reasonably suggests in *The Woman in White* that the laws are made by and for the lobbies of Rank and Success. We hear by way of preface that the novel owes its existence to the law's being "the pre-engaged servant of the long purse", leaving the villainies of Fosco and Sir Percival to be told for the first time. Social convention and the law are Fosco's passive accomplices in Laura's "death", and Hartright is constrained to serve as a self-appointed Nemesis in the manner of Pesca's revolutionary league, one of whose agents executes Fosco in Paris. We are warned by the solicitor Gilmore of the

need to master the legal complexities governing the disposal of
Laura's fortune to understand the novel, and the tendency of the
sensation novel's lingering over legal detail is to prompt the
reader to some such reflection as Thackeray's in *Vanity Fair*:

> "there must be classes—there must be rich and poor", Dives says,
> smacking his claret (it is well if he even sends the broken meat
> out to Lazarus sitting under the window). Very true; but think how
> mysterious and often unaccountable it is—that lottery of life
> which gives to this man the purple and fine linen and sends to the
> other rags for garments and dogs for comforters.

With property-law seeming to display a random intricacy, the
social order is dissociated from a providential order. Dickens'
Great Expectations (1860–61) was influenced by *The Woman in
White* and read as a sensation novel. After the convict, Mag-
witch, has used his Australian fortune to make Pip a gentle-
man, the gentlemanly ideal is related to conduct rather than class.
  The campaign for free trade in land arose from the Anti-Corn
Law movement, and expressed middle-class hostility towards an
idle aristocracy, whose estates were preserved by the "pressure
of feudal law", and in defiance of economic law. The abolition
of the estates was a radical means towards the destruction of
the aristocratic ruling class. Bright, remarks John Vincent, was
"one of the earliest leaders to educate the public mind in the
importance of the land system and the land laws and their opera-
tion on everyday life, and to inculcate a sense that these laws
were affected by the political structure of the country and might,
with advantage, be changed". In *Felix Holt*, the complexities of
property law, much dwelt upon in the novel, finally establish
Esther Lyon as heiress to Transome Court. It is an incongruous position for the adopted daughter of the local minister.
As in the sensation novels, the irrationality of the law suggests
that what divides rich and poor is riches; rather than, for instance, the purer blood which was sometimes supposed (as by
Disraeli and Ruskin) to flow through aristocratic veins. Following Pip, Esther refuses to become genteel on these terms, which
are the ordinary ones, though her renunciation is less straight-
forward and less subversive than Pip's.
  Eliot was aware of the views of her friend Herbert Spencer, who

denounced the abominations and bias of the English judicature in *Social Statics* (1851), and also advocated land nationalisation. Here he was in a minority among land reformers, most of whom were devoted to the principle of private property, and wished only to spread the ownership. Peel's conversion to the League's opinion of the Corn Laws had taken the steam out of land reform in the 1840s, but there was a delayed response to the teachings of Cobden and Bright in the mid-1860s, when earlier discussions of the question, including Spencer's, were reviewed afresh. Compensation was now a problem, Spencer allowed (he would have made short work of the original robbers of the human heritage), but one that should be resolved: "in our tender regard for the vested interests of the few, let us not forget that the rights of the many are in abeyance; and must remain so, as long as the earth is monopolised by individuals". This sense of contingency inspires some of the historical novels of the 1860s, as well as the sensation novels, and with varying consistency, the pressed sailors, the Sproxton miners, the Italians of the Risorgimento, even the Florentines in *Romola* are seen as characters whose lives are socially determined, but by forces no more to be taken for granted than the monopoly of the earth by individuals which dismays Spencer.

No less typically, the historical novels betray the obstinate iteration with which, according to Margaret Oliphant, men clung to the spirit of 1851 in changed circumstances. Like those mid-Victorian paintings associating all life's drama with domestic crisis and reconciliation, the literary "domestic saga" is a mark of confidence in the age in its broader aspects. By 1860, the saga had been overwhelmed by the sensation novel, but the conclusions to *A Tale of Two Cities* and *Felix Holt* are nothing if not domestic—Lucy and Darnay, Esther and Felix; and the preoccupation which a decade before had signified a sure faith in social stability is revived as though the faith were inseparable from the preoccupation. Romola ends up mothering Tito's children; and even in *Sylvia's Lovers* and *Vittoria*, there is a kind of tragic domesticity at the close, attended by a blurring of historical focus. Analysis proving uncomfortable, the novelists regress to a time when there was an absence of felt pressure to make the historical novel more than a romance. Society as portrayed in the sensation novels is both oppressive and vulnerable. In the historical novels, the more oppressive society is shown to be in the past, the more vulnerable it appears in the present, so that the non-revolutionary novelist ends anxious only to shield the shaky fabric, believing with Burke that any examination of the foundations of the constitution weakened its stability. The insistently contemporary sensation novelists were denied the leeway which the past gave to prevarication.

3

Charles Dickens:
A Tale of Two Cities (1859)

For a period so near to us as that of the great French Revolution of seventeen hundred and eighty-nine—upon which a few octogenarians can even now, as it were, lay their hand—it is surprising what a dim veil of mystery, horror, and romance seems to overhang the most awful convulsion of modern times. While barely passing away, it had of a sudden risen to those awful and majestic dimensions which it takes less imposing events centuries to acquire, and towered over those within its shadow as an awful pyramid of fire, blinding those who look. It requires no lying by, or waiting on, posterity for its proper comprehension. It may be read by its own light, and by those who run; and is as about intelligible at this hour as it is ever likely to be. It is felt instinctively: and those whose sense is slow, may have it quickened by Mr Carlyle's flaming torch—flaring terribly through the night. He might have been looking on in the crowd during that wild night march to Versailles, or standing at the inn door in the little French posting town, as the sun went down, waiting wearily for the heavy berline to come up. Marvellous lurid torch that of his. Pen dipped in red and fire, glowing like phosphoric writing. His history of the French Revolution, the most extraordinary book, to our thinking, in its wonderful force, picturesqueness, and condensation, ever written by mere man. There is other subsidiary light, too, for such as look back—light from tens of thousands of pamphlets, broadsides, handbills—all honest, racy of the time, writ by furious hearts, by hands trembling with frensy and excitement—hands streaked with blood and dust of the guillotine: read by mad wolfish eyes at street corners on the step of the scaffold by lamplight. Hawked about, too, by hoarse-mouthed men and women, to such horrible tune as Le Pere Duchesne est terriblement enragé aujourd'hur. An awful, repulsive cloud, darkening the air for such as look back at it. Vast shower of ribaldry, insane songs, diatribe, declamation —all shot up from that glowing crater. An inexhaustible study!

The long quotation is from a *Household Words* article, "The Eve of a Revolution", which appeared in June 1858. Dickens was a selective editor, and it may be assumed that the attitudes expressed in the article, one of a series on the French Revolution in *Household Words* in the late 1850s, coincided with his own view. Those who run may read the Revolution—or the slow may read it in Mr Carlyle's book. Dickens felt that to challenge Carlyle's evaluation would be less than modest: "It has been one of my hopes to add something to the popular and picturesque means of understanding that terrible time, though no one can hope to add anything to the philosophy of Mr Carlyle's wonderful book." And yet, according to *Household Words*, the Revolution remained "an inexhaustible study". In England, despite John Wilson Croker's research, the awful dimensions of the Revolution discouraged scholarly investigation. Carlyle, in 1837, remarked of his countrymen's revolutionary studies that "he who wishes to know how a solid *Custos rotulorum*, speculating over his port after dinner, interprets the phenomena of contemporary universal history, may look in these books: he who does not wish that, need not look"; and Carlyle himself never found time to visit Paris. Still, his version of the Revolution was sufficient unto the age. To look minutely into the phenomenon still haunting Europe was to go blind in the awful pyramid of fire.

Written in the years 1857–59, *A Tale of Two Cities* was as much a tract for the times as Carlyle's history, published twenty years before. The revolutions of 1848, and subsequent events, particularly in France, aroused insatiable interest in the circumstances of the first French Revolution. G. H. Lewes seized the opportunity to publish in 1849 a popular biography of Robespierre, since the February revolution had once more brought his "name and doctrines into alarming prominence". In September 1851, the historian Croker described revolution as

the one great subject that now occupies and agitates throughout Europe—but especially in France and England—the pens of all who write—the passions of all who feel, and the earnest and anxious thoughts of all who concern themselves about either the political or social systems under which we live or *are to live*. To advocate or to deprecate—to forward or to retard—to applaud for imitation or to expose *in terrorem* the progress of Revolution—such, wherever and to whatever extent a political press exists, is now its almost exclusive occupation.

The Revolution was painfully contemporary history for Dickens: "I have so far verified what is done and suffered in these pages, as that I have certainly done and suffered it all myself." Carlyle's work, and that of the French historian Michelet, were also composed in emotional turmoil. To Carlyle, the history was "a wild savage book, itself a kind of French Revolution", while Michelet interrupted his labours to inform a correspondent,

> I am accomplishing here the extremely tough task of reliving, reconstituting and suffering the Revolution. I have just gone through *September* and all the terrors of death; massacred at the Abbaye, I am on the way to the revolutionary tribunal, that is to say, to the guillotine.[1]

Still, the received version of the Revolution—that "awful, repulsive cloud", detached from the world—allowed English historians and historical novelists an escape from suffering. On the one hand, the Revolution was vital prehistory, and Dickens must write a novel warning his generation not to provoke the English sansculottes. On the other, it was an historical monstrosity, incapable of breeding. *A Tale of Two Cities* wavers between the two positions and gradually settles for the more comfortable. In April 1855, Dickens had written:

> I believe the discontent to be so much the worse for smouldering instead of blazing openly, that it is extremely like the general mind of France before the breaking out of the first Revolution, and is in danger of being turned by any one of a thousand accidents . . . into such a devil of a conflagration as never has been beheld since.

In 1857, he thought "the political signs of the times to be just about as bad as the spirit of the people will admit of their

[1] Edmund Wilson's translation in *To the Finland Station*, 1941, p. 25.

being", and expected the next dose of cholera to make "such a shake in this country as never was seen on Earth since Samson pulled the temple down upon his head". Dickens' subject was all too relevant to the age, and could not be treated as an "inexhaustible study". Revolutionary militancy, once described, is abstracted from its antecedents: England has nothing to learn from a freakish occurrence, and the novel's admonitory thesis is nullified. The opening pages argue not only that late eighteenth-century England was in many ways very like pre-revolutionary France, but also that England has not changed much since. On the final page, the prophetic Sidney Carton sees France "making expiation for itself", and the Manettes "peaceful, useful, prosperous and happy" in England.

Dickens takes refuge in the dogma of national characteristics. The English need not worry about revolutions in France because the French are the sort of people who are always having revolutions. A main reason for the warmth with which Tocqueville's *L'Ancien Régime et la Révolution* was greeted in England in 1856 was that he made such evasion respectable. Tocqueville's book was influenced by the experience of the June Days of 1848. The heroic People of Michelet's *Histoire de la Révolution Française* (1847) had materialised as the turbulent proletariats of the great cities of Europe. Tocqueville had seen the first essay at social revolution repressed with a savagery that made the Paris Terror seem a mild affair, and Louis Bonaparte elevated to the presidency on a tide of popular enthusiasm in the plebiscite of December 1848. While Tocqueville did insist that the march of democracy could not be stopped, and that the Revolution was still operative, its continuity, stressed in the title, with the past of the Ancien Régime was strangely qualified:

> but for the antecedent circumstances described in this book, the French would never have embarked on it; yet we must recognise that although their effect was cumulative and overwhelming, they would not have sufficed to lead to such a drastic revolution elsewhere than in France.[2]

The conceding of significance to national character gratified reviewers eager to take the concession as the book's moral, and the

[2] Stuart Gilbert's translation.

86

Westminster blithely concluded "with the author, that no people but the French could have made such a Revolution, so sudden, so violent, so full of contradictions". *Household Words* had not waited for Tocqueville to justify English complacency, and the article "Liberty, Equality, Fraternity, and Musketry" of 1851 relates to the final escape from revolutionary France in *A Tale of Two Cities*. The author crosses the channel on a sight-seeing tour, and is glad to return in one piece.

> As I saw the last cocked hat of the last gendarme disappear with the receding pier at Havre, a pleasant vision of the blue-coats, oilskin hats, and lettered collars of the land I was going to, swam before my eyes; and, I must say that, descending the companion-ladder, I thanked Heaven I was an Englishman.

In the 1853 article, "Perfidious Patmos", it is claimed that England cures exiles of rancour: "the very climate seems to have a soothing and mollifying influence on the most savage foreign natures". But the tone of the articles is not quite that permeating the conclusion of *A Tale of Two Cities*. *Household Words* in the early 1850s is John Bullish, but by the time of the novel, theories of national character are respectable intellectual currency, and the authenticity of that character can be quietly assumed.

Despite Tocqueville, the press in the late 1850s still wrote of the first French Revolution in cautionary terms, though the precise nature of the warning was debatable: either there would be revolution if parliamentary reform were conceded, or there would be if it were not. The English historians of the Revolution upheld the first position, and for Croker, Alison and Smyth, the men of 1789 were as guilty as those of 1793. The Reign of Terror was the natural and inevitable consequence of the opening of the floodgates. In January 1859, the *Quarterly* thought Bright's plan for the revision of the franchise a revolutionary project, which would turn the whole order of things upside down. Drily, Whitwell Elwin remarked that "the scheme was tried in France, and all the world knows with what result". In 1858, *The Times* was invoking "the dreadful glare of '89, the horrors of '93", making the usual point that if reform in the late 1850s seemed plain sailing, so had it in France in 1789. The opponents of reform were fond of pointing to the despotism of Louis Bonaparte as the necessary culmination of popular rule. According to W. E. Aytoun, writing in *Blackwoods* in 1859, the Emperor was what the French had earned by "practically carrying into effect those very doctrines which Mr Bright and his followers advocate": breaking down ancient landmarks, abolishing aristocracy, elevating democracy. The reformers, for their part, were capable of paying the guardians of the floodgates the same revolutionary compliment. *The Times* was opportunist as always, and while one month it might preen itself and the country generally on the striking absence of masses with fiery eyes in the tradition of 1831, the least agitation converted the paper to reform and the sluggards were menaced in their own coin. Only six weeks after the ironical reference to the plain sailing of '89, that argument was turned on its head and, in February 1859, readers reminded that the greatest things were done in a day: "the institutions of old France were overthrown, like the Bastile, in a moment of delirium". The moral here is to reform while times are quiet.

The invocation of the French Revolution by radicals and conservatives alike was more than a debating ploy, and denials of its relevance to England betrayed nervousness. The *Westminster* reviewer of Tocqueville is petulant: "if any man at that time had known what the French were as well as we know now, he would not have been surprised at anything that happened". The shying away from the threat of revolution in England, detectable here, is responsible for certain attitudes to the past recurrent in the literature of the period, and which have been noticed in the Introduction. In Froude's *History of England* and its reviews, the estrangement which is a feature of life in the class-divided modern city is identified with the human condition; and those cut off from their contemporaries come to feel the still greater difficulty of relating to the past as inevitable. Dickens was acutely aware of isolation and fear in the great city, and was capable of taking a detached view. It is the main force of *Little Dorrit* (1855–57) to depict the slow and tentative coming-together of humans within the city, and to deny that isolation is an inescapable condition. But Dickens' position was ambivalent: he was within the situation he described. John Forster cites a memorandum, the idea of "representing London—or Paris, or any other great place—in the new light of being actually unknown to all the people in the story, and only taking the colour of their fears and fancies and opinions". Here Dickens feels the imprisoning subjectivism bred by urban life as new and strange, but there is little indication that he will adopt a perspective; and that is because he, too, is a prisoner.

Dickens was alert not only to the divisive social forces, but also to the opposing energy of those striving to connect; and connection triumphs in the contemporary *Little Dorrit* (contemporary in that it deals with the England of his own lifetime). In *A Tale of Two Cities*, Dickens is removed from his characters, and a sense of their capacity to survive a harsh environment; and tends to accept inter-personal estrangement as the great reality.

> A wonderful fact to reflect upon, that every human creature is constituted to be that profound secret and mystery to every other. A solemn consideration, when I enter a great city by night, that every one of those darkly clustered houses encloses its own secret. . . .

This dogmatic pessimism, unchallenged within the historical novel, leads to the final sinking of history in vapid moralising, all the more incongruous since earlier Dickens has shown some precision in the delineation of a past whose main feature, admittedly, is a striking resemblance to the present. Still, the resemblance is defined and guarantees the past an exemplary status, lost later when the fog of the nineteenth century settles more densely over its prehistory.

To the Enlightenment historian who thought human nature unchanging, the past was totally familiar, and urgently relevant to the present, not as prehistory but as a casebook of examples. Such attitudes were still current in England in the 1850s, and for W. Frederick Pollock, writing in the *Quarterly* in 1858, the historian's business was to record "the great virtues and the great crimes" of distinguished men. The course of *A Tale of Two Cities* represents a progressive falling away from the Enlightenment tradition. Like the Enlightenment historians—like the English historians on the French Revolution, Croker, Smyth, Alison and Buckle—Dickens begins by taking the Revolution as exemplary. He ends by making it a special case, not because history never repeats itself, but because the revolutionaries were exceptionally wicked and moreover French.

89

Under pressure in the 1830s, historians had blurred their moral by portraying the revolutionaries as evil men, and Archibald Alison, in his *History of Europe* (1833–42), was sometimes inclined to attribute the Revolution to guilt, treachery and delusion. But with an awareness that the judgment negated the warning to his contemporaries, he could remark that historians conveying the Jacobins as "mere bloodthirsty wretches, vultures insatiate in their passion for destruction, are well-meaning and amiable, but weak and ignorant men", calculated to mislead rather than instruct future ages on the avoidance of revolution. Croker's esteem for Robespierre kept pace with his research. He had dealt scathingly with Robespierre in the *Quarterly* for September 1835, but in 1857, among his *Essays on the Early Period of the French Revolution*, treated the subject more thoroughly. Here he pointed out that the impartial praise of the pre-revolutionary sources to which he now referred was a positive indication of Robespierre's underrated abilities; and condemned previous historians who, instead of trying to clarify the obscurities of Robespierre's career, took "the easier course of finding nothing to doubt about".

Like the historians, the novelists dealing with the French Revolution were divided between its ascription to excessive wickedness and a broader historical view. Bulwer's *Zanoni* appeared in 1842, and Trollope's *La Vendée* in 1850. Bulwer weakens his polemical point against revolution in general by making a devil out of Robespierre in the way that the historians were learning to avoid, but Trollope is more sophisticated. Like *A Tale of Two Cities*, *La Vendée* is intended as a warning to the author's contemporaries: the Revolution is highly exemplary and shows the 1850s what not to do. Consistently with his main purpose, Trollope is at pains to emphasise that Robespierre was "not a thoughtless, wild fanatic". His career is a terrible instance of what happens when the populace gains political power.

In 1847, Michelet's *Histoire de la Révolution Française* appeared and, with the histories of Lamartine and Louis Blanc, was widely read in England. Michelet was influenced by the revolutionary aspirations manifested the following year, and his history exemplified the French use of a justifying determinism in the democratic cause which alarmed English historians, and helped to provoke them to the opposite extreme, an insistence on their characters' absolute moral responsibility. Michelet's method was to coin abstractions—"Le Peuple", "La Révolution"—which acquired a motive force of their own, so that many acts hitherto considered crimes could be excused in terms of these figments working out their own inexorable destiny. What Michelet unequivocally condemns in the Revolution—he does not admire the Jacobins—does not reflect on the purity of "La Révolution", or France. The abstractions of Michelet's idealism are paralleled by those which class fears imposed on Carlyle and Dickens, and William Smyth pointed out that the determinism of the French historians could be used for conservative as well as radical purposes. Still, there appeared in 1849 in the *British Quarterly Review* a percipient analysis by E. Edwards of "Historians of the first French Revolution", which exposed the basis of English hostility to the French histories. Michelet's determinism was only the overflowing of his conviction that "whatever the immediate and apparent issues of the events narrated, a grand result was being slowly but ceaselessly evolved". It was the grand result which the English historians were fearful of acknowledging; and Edwards went on to remark that Carlyle, despite stylistic resemblances to Michelet, was actually a very different case. His history was detached, ironical, disjointed, unsympathetic. "He sees in the Revolution no development of a law of progress. For him it begins with an 'Age of paper', and ends with a 'Whiff of grape-shot'."

Aware of the London slums, Carlyle acquired early the disenchantment with democracy that struck French historians after 1848, pervading Tocqueville and notably absent in Michelet. In "Signs of the Times" (1829), he wrote of a

> deep-lying struggle in the whole fabric of society; a boundless grinding collision of the New with the Old. The French Revolution, as is now visible enough, was not the parent of this mighty movement, but its offspring. . . . The final issue was not unfolded in that country: nay it is not yet anywhere unfolded.

Carlyle understands that the Revolution is no isolated calamity, product of the guilt, treachery and delusion of individuals; still, it is less firmly anchored in history than its causes, and already significance is attributed to popular movements only in so far as they are symptomatic of something else, the deep-rooted craving of the masses for paternal guidance. Ten years later, in *Chartism*, Carlyle wrote that it was no answer to call agitation "mad, incendiary, nefarious". Chartism had profound economic causes, and was provoked by the system of *laissez-faire* (what Tellson's Bank stands for in *A Tale of Two Cities*). But by 1839, Carlyle was less willing consistently to relate agitation to the social context. He generalises about "all popular commotions and maddest bellowings, from Peterloo to the Place-de-Grève itself", and his gathering retreat from the challenge of democracy is witnessed by contradictions within the essay. It is no answer to call popular commotions "mad"; and yet they may be equated with "maddest bellowings".

Carlyle's historical theory and practice were shaped by his growing conservatism. In the 1830 essay, "On History", he protested against Enlightenment historiography and wished to substitute, for the easy assumption of a constant human nature, research into the driving forces of particular epochs. He insisted that men, as well as their environment, were always changing, and commented, "when the oak-tree is felled, the whole forest echoes with it; but a hundred acorns are planted silently by some unnoticed breeze". This meant that the most important part of our history was irrecoverably lost, and put the onus on the historian to recover what he could, while he could. Progressively, Carlyle forgot the acorns and concentrated on the more accessible oak-tree.

Scott's influence was generously acknowledged. After *Waverley*, history's "faint hearsays of 'philosophy teaching by experience' will have to exchange themselves everywhere for direct inspection and embodiment. . . ." But the curiosity of the essay on "Sir Walter Scott" (1838) is that his triumphant demonstration that the past was filled by living men does not satisfy Carlyle. These living men are reified by the claim that Scott's main appeal is nostalgic: "Consider, brethren, shall we not too one day be antiques, and grow to have as quaint a costume as the rest?" Carlyle objects that the novels offer no heroic cure for the ailing modern heart; not a criticism to be levelled at his own *Past and Present* in 1843. Despite his pleas for research, it is taken for granted that the maimed records of the past will be interpreted in the light of the historian's emotions and prejudices. In the essay, he is writing on this assumption, even while praising Scott for inaugurating another kind of history; and the Waverley novels fail as great literature because they are not sufficiently encouraging.

Scott communicated the spirit of an age through analysis of popular movements, and inspired historians to do the same. Too conscious of the past's opaqueness, Carlyle could react to Scott's example only by vulgarisation. The spirit of the age was dissociated from popular life and transformed into a much more abstract *zeitgeist*, there to guide the historian when his evidence failed him. The conception of the *zeitgeist* did not evolve from research, it substituted for research; or rather, since the *zeitgeist* engendered all things, a few facts might be assumed to reveal the essence of great events. In *The French Revolution* (1837), Carlyle responds to the fall of the universally-detested Bastille by lamenting that men have died in the process, and his moral indignation becomes an index of the event. Reviewing the book, Mazzini wrote truly that Carlyle did "not recognise in a people any collective life or collective aim. He recognises only individuals. For him, therefore, there is not and cannot be any intelligible chain of connection between cause and effect". Carlyle's quest after direct inspection and embodiment was a limited success. His characterisation of individuals was frequently acute, but of the collective movement he could embody only his own prejudices.

Writing *The French Revolution*, Carlyle was less sceptical about the accessibility of historical evidence than convinced that some data was not worth the gathering. Like Michelet, he treats summarily the events preceding the outbreak of revolution, when the daemonic suddenly erupts against the spurious, as, in Michelet, good erupts against the evil of the Ancient Regime. In "On History", Carlyle insisted that history was composed of innumerable biographies. The Ancient Regime treats the people as "masses", and Carlyle pleads for historical empathy: "masses indeed: and yet, singular to say, if, with an effort of imagination, thou follow them, over broad France, into their garrets and hutches, the masses consist of all units". What Carlyle asks of the reader is the ideal which he cannot realise as an historian. Having described the storming of the Bastille, he forgets that the Revolution is made by individuals, and lapses into empty abstraction, denouncing the fever-frenzies of Anarchy enveloping the world. He deals with units only in isolation, and the units are always the "great men", great because emancipated from a mediocre environment. Like the Revolution, the great man rises up to announce that shams shall be no more, and between shams and reality can be no interaction. Lacking antecedents, the Revolution's course is credited to "necessity". That of the French historians (especially Michelet) made the revolutionaries the puppets of moral abstractions; Carlyle's, typically English, makes them the puppets of human nature, degraded to the brutish once the floodgates are opened.

Carlyle's views on the Revolution cannot be systematised. He was proud of his reputation as its most impartial historian, but there is more contradiction than impartiality. He criticises his predecessors for recording the Reign of Terror in hysterics, and then explains the Terror by commenting that in History as in Nature, certain periods are covered over by "Darkness and the mystery of horrid cruelty". The autonomy that the forces of madness come to exercise suggests Carlyle's awareness that the Revolution was generating its own momentum; and significantly, his loathing for the Radicals grew as he wrote the book. Hedva Ben-Israel remarks of the historian, William Smyth, that "if contemporary conditions drove him to the study of the Revolution, it is even more obvious how much this study helped to formulate his political opinions and to intensify the process of his growing conservatism". The same is true of Carlyle, and also of Dickens in *A Tale of Two Cities*. For both, the experience of writing on the Revolution showed that their liberalism was not proof against the description of class war.

A Tale of Two Cities was published in 1859, twenty-two years after Carlyle's history. Dickens' letters show an urgency in their forebodings of civil conflict lacking in Carlyle's essays, and cannot be suspected of indulging in revolutionary prophecy to speed reform. Apprehension of the London sansculottes was one reason why his account was remoter than Carlyle's from the historical actuality of the French Revolution. Defensively, and more than his mentor, he too missed the collective life or aim and saw only individuals. Though Carlyle diverts attention immediately afterwards, during the storming, his eye is on the Bastille:

At every street-barricade, there whirls simmering a minor whirl-pool,—strengthening the barricade, since God knows what is coming; and all minor whirlpools play distractedly into that grand Fire-Mahlstrom which is lashing round the Bastille.

Whole sentences in A Tale of Two Cities are very close to Carlyle, except for Dickens' more profound inclination to subordinate the historical event to the illumination of private character. His narrative of the storming concentrates not on the Bastille, but Defarge:

> As a whirlpool of boiling waters has a centre point, so, all this raging circled round Defarge's wine-shop, and every human drop in the caldron had a tendency to be sucked towards the vortex where Defarge himself, already begrimed with gunpowder and sweat, issued orders. . . .

Dickens the novelist might seem to be realising the Revolution through its impact on the individual, but he rather implies that Defarge is the guiding force of the Revolution. The conversion of Carlyle's vibrant metaphor to a laboured simile suggests the difficulty with which Dickens dramatised his dubious version of events. The revolutionary crowd which is active in Carlyle ("whirls simmering", "play distractedly", "lashing") is acted upon in Dickens. Consistently, Carlyle's irony is subdued to the hysteria of the individual as victim, the novelist's response to his projection into the past. Madame Defarge's Bacchantes substitute for the "one woman (with her sweetheart), and one Turk" who, according to Carlyle, joined the sansculottes in storming the Bastille. The dialogue is bizarre throughout the novel, but Madame Defarge says some extraordinary things because she is a mad puppet talking to herself; she enjoys the splendid isolation which is Darnay's, when he crosses to Paris during the Terror in the hope of restraining the revolutionary fury. Amongst the crowd, Defarge is as helpless "as if he had been struggling in the surf at the South Sea": even the arch-instigator is estranged from the struggle at hand. The idea of the crowd as a natural force is narrowed down until emphasis falls only on the cruelty of nature, and the history becomes increasingly deterministic, helping Dickens to draw his generalised moral about revolutions.

In the opening pages of A Tale of Two Cities, Dickens sees little to choose between the condition of pre-revolutionary France and that of England in the late eighteenth century; or of England in the

1850s. Fitzjames Stephen's review missed the point by implying that the automatic sneer at the past was characteristic of the novel, despite the odd hint of Victorian complacence. Commonly derived from the French Revolution was the lesson of what happened when a country's aristocracy abjured its responsibilities and ceased to govern, and reviewing Tocqueville's account in the *Edinburgh*, W. R. Greg found a picture "of that destruction of all *class cohesion*—that dissolution of the entire nation into a mere crowd of unconnected units—which made the convulsion, when it did come, utterly unopposed and irresistible. . . ." Dickens' England in the 1780s is precisely a "crowd of unconnected units", with no one playing a defined social role. "The highwayman in the dark was a City tradesman in the light", and the ease of the transition suggests a resemblance between the two occupations. The social fabric, so far from being settled for ever, is ripe for violent change.

At this point, Dickens is not merely attacking harsh rulers who ought to be more charitable. For Carlyle in *Chartism*, democracy was "the consummation of No-government and *Laissez-faire*". In the novel, Jerry Cruncher thinks of his occupation and tells himself, "you'd be in a Blazing bad way, if recalling to life was to come into fashion. . . ."; but as well as being a body-snatcher, Jerry is also a messenger for Tellson's Bank, which equally would be in a bad way. The society trusting its wealth to Tellson's vaults provides dead bodies in plenty for Jerry to dig up again. The great keys of the underground strongrooms at Tellson's correspond to those of the Bastille; and as the Bastille is the symbol of oppression in France, so is Tellson's in England. Its broad social tendency is reflected in the depersonalisation of its employees: Lorry's life is spent "turning an immense pecuniary mangle". Dickens hints that if oppression continues, there will be a storming of Tellson's, whose great keys will open the vaults for good.

Dickens' assault on the system of *laissez-faire* does not, however, survive his descriptions of revolution in France. He is induced to settle for any society that is non-revolutionary, forgetting that the old regime in England had seemed patently to invite revolution. Gradually, Lorry becomes an unequivocally positive figure; at first because, despite his disclaimers, he unites "friendship", "interest", and "sentiment" with banking. Later, Lorry's virtue is inseparable from his attachment to Tellson's. During the

Revolution, he occupies rooms in the Parisian branch of the bank, "in his fidelity to the House of which he had grown to be a part, like a strong root-ivy". The root-ivy simile looks sinister, but the undertones conflict with Dickens' intended meaning, and are a confused remembrance of the days when Tellson's itself seemed a decidedly sinister institution. What Tellson's stands for in England is made plain after the outbreak of revolution, when the aristocratic emigrées flee there as to a natural haven. It is nevertheless at this stage that Dickens begins to approve of the bank. He has stressed that England has been brought close to revolution by political and economic reaction; yet when (for Dickens) a roughly similar state of affairs has provoked revolution in France, Tellson's can somehow be portrayed as a source of social stability.

Though the doctor has been victimised by the old regime in France, the Manettes' safety is linked with that of the money in Tellson's vaults, which is safe enough under Lorry's guardianship. They have not always enjoyed such security. The house in Soho had been "a very harbour from the raging streets", but Dickens associates the wreaths of dust in Soho with those raised by the Parisian sansculottes. Gradually, he identifies with that British orthodoxy regarding the Revolution as "the one only harvest ever known under the skies that had not been sown", a random occurrence bearing no warning for England. He continues to state that the revolution is the product of intolerable oppression, but the tale movies in another direction. The career of Miss Pross is significant. Her chauvinism begins as a joke, more John Bullish than the articles on France in *Household Words*. When she asks why providence should have cast her lot in an island if she was intended to cross the sea, Dickens is being gently satirical; less gently, he satirises those claiming their social rank from providence. But at the end of the novel, in the woman-to-woman struggle with Madame Defarge, Miss Pross's chauvinism is justified: her courage is specifically English, "a courage that Madame Defarge so little comprehended as to mistake for weakness". Miss Pross becomes an agent of the derided providence, and writing to Bulwer in 1860, Dickens gravely defended her enemy's "accidental" death.

Where the accident is inseparable from the passion and action of the character; where it is strictly consistent with the whole design, and arises out of some culminating proceeding on the part of the character which the whole story has led up to, it seems to me to become, as it were, an act of divine justice.

Miss Pross literally harbours Lucie Manette from the raging streets. Embodied in Madame Defarge, the Revolution derives less from oppression than French depravity, which is no match for English virtue.

At the beginning of the novel, Dickens sees the Revolution as a rebuff to middle-class ideology. His scorn for the mentality (Lorry's) vindicating business as "a very good thing, and a very respectable thing", is reminiscent of Carlyle's strictures on the limitations of the Girondins. But Dickens cannot sympathise with the actual revolutionaries whom he portrays, and tells us why in his account of Madame Defarge:

> . . . the troubled time would have heaved her up, under any circumstances. But, imbued from her childhood with a brooding sense of wrong, and an inveterate hatred of a class, opportunity had developed her into a tigress.

Madame Defarge can be excused for being revolutionary in a general kind of way, but not for her class ideology, whose violence provokes a corresponding violence in Dickens. The blood-smeared eyes of the sansculottes sharpening their weapons in Tellson's yard are "eyes which any unbrutalised beholder would have given twenty years of life, to petrify with a well-directed gun". "Unbrutalised" reads ironically, and there is more irony if we remember the petrified Monseigneur. Dickens now prefers the stony hearts of the aristocracy to the revolutionary crowd, and would play the Gorgon with history as the French aristocrats tried to do.

Early in the novel, since the ruling class has reneged on its responsibilities, virtue is not a connotation of fine dress. Dickens' later tendency, to assume that clothes make the man, derives from the persuasion that nations must be composed of unconnected units, each one a "profound secret and mystery to every other". Dickens becomes indignant with revolutionary innovations. From the look of the tribunal, he comments, it would seem that "the felons were trying the honest men". The moral order turned upside down will be that wherein "honest" justice is meted out to felons; presumably the judicial norm in non-revolutionary society. Darnay has contrary experience of the English bench. Oddly, though, he recoils from the aristocrats in La Force through an "instinctive association of prisoners with shameful crime and disgrace". Sympathy with the victims of revolution leads Dickens to share with Darnay the conventional prejudice which has been invalidated.

Sydney Carton's career is problematic: he is clearly a failure, but Dickens sometimes seems to be asking whether in such a society as Carton finds himself, it is not a virtue to be a failure. While he may be simply weak, "the man of good abilities and good emotions, incapable of their directed exercise", the kind of strength leading to success is exemplified in Stryver:

> anybody who had seen him projecting himself into Soho while he was yet on the Saint Dunstan's side of Temple Bar, bursting into his full-blown way along the pavement, to the jostlement of all weaker people, might have seen how safe and strong he was.

Tellson's strongrooms are also "safe, and strong, and sound, and still"; and the stillness here is an emblem of the ultimate stultification of Stryver's bustling activity. Stryver's success as a lawyer is based on the exploitation of the weak Carton, while his own contribution to the partnership is to be "glib", "unscrupulous", "ready" and "bold". These business virtues combine with a resentment of democratic movements threatening to jeopardise his opulent living, and at Tellson's, he broaches to the emigrées his plans for "blowing the people up and exterminating them from the face of the earth. . . ." Stryver's disposition towards the French revolutionaries is shared by Carton as he ceases to be the mere jackal. While Madame Defarge points him to the National Palace, Carton reflects that "it might be a good deed to seize that arm, lift it, and strike under it sharp and deep". In the face of revolution, Carton is as willing to resort to repressive brutality as any *homme sensible*, and his progressive ennoblement in the novel cannot be dissociated from his acquisition of bourgeois traits. Yet once, Carton had been seen not only as weak (that is one explanation), but also as among the numerous victims of a ruthlessly competitive society. "And whose fault was that?" asks Stryver, when Carton complains of his failure. Carton feels that it was Stryver's, whose "driving and riving and shouldering and pressing" forced his partner to a self-preserving "rust and repose".

Carton also competes, unsuccessfully, with Charles Darnay for the love of Lucie Manette, and his pining for the middle-class doll undercuts his subversive potential from early on. It is implied that his failure in love is inevitable, but the pining over Lucie is not convincing: there are qualities in the Carton who talks back to Stryver which suggest more backbone. Perhaps, and without slighting Lucie, Dickens was hinting that domestic content depended on worldly fortune; and that in the society he was treating, this was not for everybody. Lucie rejects Stryver, too, while Darnay is the happy medium: undoubtedly successful, but earning his modest income conscientiously as a private tutor. What is important in Carton's case is that the rebel should die at the hands of the revolutionaries on behalf of Lucie and the middle-class family, and if the situation seems contrived, that is all to the point. Anyway, the enigmas of Carton's career—the strained progress from rebel to revolutionary victim, and the dubious values which accompany his ennoblement—are shelved at his death, along with other problems which the historical novel has raised, not always intentionally. If Carton has been corrupted within history (as Dickens may have sensed), his death is a comprehensive retreat from the world's stain. As the guillotine falls,

> the murmuring of many voices, the upturning of many faces, the pressing on of many footsteps in the outskirts of the crowd, so that it swells forward in a mass, like one great heave of water, all flashes away.

At the end, Carton prophesies a secure and happy England without relation to the England presented earlier; nor, one would have thought, did the France of 1859 merit his optimism.

It is the passivity of the future state which is insisted upon, and Carton's death is the logical consummation of a novel increasingly stressing the blessings of inertia as the Revolution proceeds. Activity (movement in history) is associated with corruption, passivity with preserved innocence. Lorry, praised as the best possible man "to hold fast by what Tellson's had in its keeping, and to hold his peace", is beyond criticism because he refuses to enter the historical argument. History begins with the Fall, the collapse of timeless innocence, and the Carmagnole is "emphatically a fallen sport": but as the dance passes, leaving Lucie frightened and bewildered, "the feathery snow fell as quietly and lay as white and soft, as if it had never been". Quietly, the snow obliterates the marks of history, and returns the world to a uniform white. This, rather than the fallen historical world of Madame Defarge, is Lucie's habitat. Before becoming respectable, Carton called her a doll; accurately since, although Lucie marries and has several children, she never acquires a character. Throughout, she enjoys the immunity to time which England offers her at the close.

To state mechanically what is mechanically executed, the theme of resurrection pervades the novel. Dr Manette is saved from burial alive in the Bastille, but has gone mad, and needs Lucie's loving care to revive his senses. Darnay is twice rescued by Sydney Carton from what seems certain death, in London and Paris, and Jerry Cruncher is a "Resurrection-man", or body-snatcher. There are two mock funerals, those of Cly, the Old Bailey spy, and Foulon, who causes a servant to be buried in his stead and is "recalled to life" only to be slaughtered by the Parisian crowd. Resurrection suggests a possible moral resurgence, and early in the novel, the idea of that resurgence is inseparable from social change. Dickens is curiously honest about Dr Manette's second resurrection, the restoration to mental health. "In a mysterious and guilty manner", Lorry hacks to pieces the shoemaker's bench, while Miss Pross holds the candle "as if she were assisting at a murder": their secret destruction seems like "a horrible crime", but the patient cannot be cured otherwise. Lorry's and Miss Pross's demolition of the momentoes of the Bastille precedes its razing by the revolutionaries.

Later in A Tale of Two Cities, destruction and secrecy are simply wicked. Resurrection assumes exclusively Christian connotations, and as Carton prepares to die to save Darnay, the words of the Anglican burial service recur to his mind. The Christian position is the same as Carlyle's in "Signs of the Times": "to reform a world, to reform a nation, no wise man will undertake; and all but foolish men know, that the only solid, though a far slower reformation, is what each begins and perfects on *himself*". Dickens is forced to such modest wisdom through his fear of revolution in England, and yet in a way he is still being honest. Carton yearns less for resurrection than the "far, far better rest". Finally, the escape from history is enough.

4

Popular Politics in George Eliot's Historical Novels of the 1860s

Romola (1863) deals with the rise and fall of Savonarola in Florence in the 1490s; *Felix Holt the Radical* (1866) is set in England in the era of the first Reform Act. It is paradoxical that while Elizabeth Gaskell, whose private life was impeccable and who disapproved of those who flouted convention, wrote novels challenging the cherished assumptions of her time, George Eliot, privately a rebel, should be so apprehensive of the democratic equality which, according to Tocqueville, every event and every man was helping along, that in *Romola* and *Felix Holt*, she argues that the evolution of man's moral nature, the only true progress, is independent of politics. Mrs Gaskell wished that George Eliot *was* the Mrs Lewes she styled herself. If Gaskell's defined role as daughter and wife to Unitarian ministers helped her to view society dispassionately, perhaps the insecurity which was the price of Eliot's defiance made her all the more nervous of the historical challenge to the established order.

Eliot did not, like Gaskell, and also like Ruskin whose *Stones of Venice* (1851–53) was an important influence on *Romola* and *Felix Holt*, view the rise of the middle-class sensibility as an event in history. Her novels, products of a later phase of development, show how she identified bourgeois with human consciousness. They abound in asides to a known kind of reader, and do not portray working people below, say, the rank of Caleb Garth in *Middlemarch* as convincing individuals. The identification meant that she did not anticipate a ruling-class "change of heart", and a virtue of inability to see herself as a character in history was that her novels were spared the simplistic resolutions of social problems, marring *Mary Barton* and *North and South*. In both *Romola* and *Felix Holt*, however, the alternative is to dissipate the problems by sleights of hand which embarrass her less than Dickens, who hides the traces of the Carmagnole with a coy snowstorm.

There is a critical consensus that *Romola* is a failure. F. R. Leavis rightly complains that the novel is all analysis and no presence, and this is the general verdict. Still, *Romola* remains of interest for what it conveys of the perplexities of the liberal-conservative intellectual in the 1860s, though not for its study of fifteenth-century Florence.

Joan Bennett remarks that probably, once Eliot "had chosen an historical subject from the remote past, she was bound to fail. . . ."[1] This is partly true; but Scott's medieval novels set out to convey past conflicts in a way that is never attempted in *Romola*, and more than perversity doomed Eliot to write a novel with a Renaissance setting. In a valuable dissertation on *Romola*, G. A. Santangelo notes affinities with the historiography of Ruskin, Comte and others, without relating these affinities to the novel's failure, which is taken for granted. Of course, Eliot's view of the past, and contemporary views which were congenial to her, are integral to *Romola*'s failure as an historical novel. Relating *Adam Bede* (1859) to the moral evolutionism of Herbert Spencer's *Social Statics* (1851), John Goode writes that he is "not arguing that *Adam Bede* is a fictional version of Herbert Spencer, but that the concrete realization of the empirical vision exists in tension with the historically specific ideology which shapes it".[2] *Romola*, set in the 1490s instead of the 1790s, is very close to a fictional version of Spencer, Comte and Ruskin: the empirical vision dulls with distance. But we need not regard Eliot's choice of the Florentine subject as an aberration. Eliot is writing a Renaissance novel not, like Bulwer and his disciples, in an attempt to recapture the spirit of former centuries, but on the contrary, to demonstrate that there is no historical uniqueness to strive after. She is putting herself under obligation to fail as an historical novelist.

In *Felix Holt*, George Eliot was writing about the 1830s, the

[1] *George Eliot: Her Mind and Art*, 1948, p. 150
[2] *Critical Essays on George Eliot*, 1970, p. 36.

time of her own childhood, and she is too close to the age not to approach it empirically. The early chapters create Holt as a character in history, possessing historical awareness, and Mrs Transome's story does more than point the generalised moral extracted by Arnold Kettle, that "we get nothing on the cheap in this severe world and no past action is obliterated".[3] Ruskin's discussion of egoism as a class attribute is as important to *Felix Holt* as to *Romola*; and it is true of both novels that the tendency induced in Ruskin, the great analyst of *laissez-faire*, by his mistrust of the workers, to translate social disparities into moral issues for the upper-class conscience, eases Eliot's retreat to a purely private realm. In *Felix Holt*, however, her retreat is more palpably evasive, since she has not worked abstractedly. The course of *Romola* is perfectly consistent. But we cannot explain why Holt, who has resolved to leave Treby and preach to the masses, finally leaves to do nothing of the kind, or why the scathing critique of the law is dropped once it appears as a defence against popular violence, if we see Eliot writing merely as the detached Spencerian or Comtist. *Felix Holt*, like *A Tale of Two Cities* and unlike *Romola*, acquires a momentum of its own.

"Romola"

There is, Eliot writes in the Proem to *Romola*, "a likeness in human building that will be broader and deeper than all possible change": her tone anticipates acquiescence, and the sentiment pervades the novel. Eliot's "local colouring" in *Romola* is precisely that. The superficial differences between the fifteenth and nineteenth centuries are the backcloth to events, and the seizing of the "typical" moment means a pause in the narrative. The justification of the tedious Chapter XVI, "A Florentine Joke", is its illustration of "a scene such as Florentines loved".

Eliot's movement from the empirical vision of her more nearly contemporary historical novel, *Adam Bede*, was ratified by the "social-political-conservatism" which she shared with Riehl. Reviewing his *Natural History of German Life* in 1856, Eliot wrote that the

[3] *ibid.*, p. 106.

vital connection with the past is much more vividly felt on the Continent than in England, where we have to recall it by an effort of memory and reflection; for though our English life is in its core intensely traditional, Protestantism and commerce have modernized the face of the land and the aspects of society in a far greater degree than in any continental society. . . .

Eliot is arguing that the evolutionary progress of mankind is independent of such historical phenomena. In *Adam Bede*, as John Goode notes, the modernising influences are present only for their superficiality to be exposed. Eliot set *Romola* in Renaissance Florence partly because the vote's proven meaninglessness in the closed community would indicate its irrelevance in nineteenth-century England, where the chance to be elected was confined to an exclusive sect; and also to pursue her moral-evolutionary thesis undistracted by peripheral modernisation. In *Romola*, all value is located in the individual divorced from a society which there is no serious attempt to portray, and what might seem a characteristic disjunction of the historical romance is carefully contrived. It is transferred to the succeeding novels, where the missions of Felix Holt and Daniel Deronda are isolated from a more immediate social context.

Abandoned by Bulwer after *Harold* in 1848, the historical romance conveyed religious propaganda in the 1850s and more general views about politics and society in the next decade. Cynicism about the possibility of recapturing the past pervaded G. H. Lewes' essay on "Historical Romance", written in 1846, where his critical theory of the romance preluded *Romola*. Lewes insisted that the historical novel should aim both at the "accurate historical picture" and "aesthetic truth"; and the aesthetic truth would be modern moral truth (justifying historical anachronism) rather than truth to history. There were alternative methods by which the novelist might embark on his dual task:

> either he may depict the moral peculiarities of the epoch in his subordinate characters, while preserving the modern nature of his heroes,—and then his heroes will simply be men in advance of their age; or he may exhibit the moral peculiarities of the epoch in his heroes, and by showing how these men partook of the failings and errors of their age, draw a valuable lesson from the exhibition; and

then we shall have a picture of moral greatness somewhat modified
by the element in which it moved.

Lewes wrote that it did not much matter which method was
chosen, so long as consistency was maintained. Scott, we are told,
did well to adopt the first course, safer for those ungifted with
powers of mental analysis; and the misreading of Scott, whose
heroes are modern only in their historical context, is significant.
But the first option was no more remote from the classical historical novel than the second, which conceived the past in terms
of failings and errors detracting from the moral greatness to be
achieved in the present. In *Romola*, the subordinate characters
reflect "the mortal peculiarities of the epoch", as in the episode of
the Florentine joke. Meanwhile, Eliot follows one of Lewes' options
on heroic characterisation for Romola, and the other for Savonarola. The heroine is in advance of her age, and so can appeal to
nineteenth-century sympathies. Savonarola, however, is "a picture
of moral greatness somewhat modified by the element in which it
moved": an element with which Romola has little to do.

Her review of Charles Kingsley's *Westward Ho!* (1855) shows
that George Eliot shared Lewes' conception of the historical novel:

> hardly any period could furnish a happier subject for an historical
> fiction than the one Mr Kingsley has here chosen. It is unhackneyed,
> and it is unsurpassed in the grandeur of its moral elements, and
> the picturesqueness and the romance of its manners and events.

While the "moral elements" might be integral to the Elizabethan
period, they are markedly isolated from the "manners and events"
of the age; which are themselves reduced to mere "picturesqueness" and "romance". Condemning, in 1846, the old firm of Harrison Ainsworth, G. P. R. James and Bulwer, Lewes anticipated the
attributes of the historical novel of the 1860s and later. Here,
the "history", however deeply researched in an antiquarian spirit,
is no more than backcloth to the preconceived modern message.
While the Waverley novels deal with historical conflict, in *Romola*
or *The Cloister and the Hearth*, stranded moderns conflict with
their unaccustomed surroundings. *Romola* does relate to a central
tradition of Renaissance historiography, and in his review, R. H.
Hutton was right in thinking that Eliot took Florentine history

seriously. But it is there in *Romola* only for the exposure of the superficiality of historical change.

Roscoe's *Life of Lorenzo de Medici* was published in 1795, and his account of the Renaissance soon dated. Unlike the nineteenth-century historians who pictured Florence pining under a Medici tyranny, Roscoe hero-worshipped Lorenzo, and derived the cultural renaissance from thriving civil liberties: "Florence, like a sheltered garden in the opening of spring, re-echoed with the earliest sounds of returning animation". Adulation of Lorenzo meant that Savonarola, champion of popular freedom, appeared as a morose and insolent fanatic. We read in her diary that George Eliot "continued Roscoe, with much disgust at his shallowness and folly".

Following Roscoe's biography, there was less inclination amongst historians of the Renaissance to idealise either the society or the culture. In Ruskin's *Stones of Venice*, the Renaissance garden was seen as the paradise of a privileged few. The essence of Gothic architecture had been its predilection for "quaint fancy, rich ornament, bright colour, something that shows a sympathy with men of ordinary hearts"; but the architecture of the Renaissance was "rigid, cold, inhuman". Versailles, apotheosis of Renaissance luxury, had earned revolution. English industrial society in the nineteenth century derived from the same poison-tree, and in his chapter on "The Nature of Gothic", Ruskin showed how the material demands of the rich were dehumanising the labour force. Popular agitation expressed the operative's sense of debasement at the performance of work which was distasteful. Taking for her hero Savonarola, Eliot was writing about the early leader of the great social movement which incorporated the French Revolution and Chartism.

Chapter XXXIX of *Romola*, "A Supper in the Rucellai Gardens", looks like a Ruskinian view of the walled garden of the ruling class in the Renaissance. But Eliot's thesis was not Ruskin's. Venerated as a teacher of "grand doctrines of truth and sincerity in art, and the nobleness and solemnity of our human life", he was also accused of "arrogant absurdity" on economic points. According to Ruskin, the millenium would be realised through the ruling class's spontaneous renunciation of the egoism by which it had been characterised since the Renaissance. In *Romola*, Eliot was bent on denying even the tenuous relation between moral attitudes and class which this pious hope implied, and seeming to accept Ruskin's interpretation of the Renaissance, wrote to expose its inadequacy.

Tito, Romola's husband, is no more filial towards his stepfather, Baldassare, than the ruling class is paternal towards the Florentines; and in his attempted revenge, Baldassare becomes a portent of the nemesis to which the ruling class is vulnerable. He walks the Rucellai Gardens in narrowing circuits, while the company inside the house, including Tito, dine off peacock's flesh, in defiance of Savonarola's teaching that "it was not the duty of the rich to be luxurious for the sake of the poor". Thwarted on this occasion, Baldassare is finally revenged when he strangles Tito on the riverbank. The Rucellai Gardens episode suggests that Tito's egoism is a class attribute, and that the feasters dread popular vengeance as much as Tito fears that of his stepfather; but the mass victims of class-egoism do not get the sympathy from Eliot which she expends on Baldassare, literally maddened by Tito's callousness. Of course, Baldassare's revenge has an irrational element. Like the crowd, he is stirred to a fever by the emotionalism of Savonarola's preaching, so that the murder serves as a terrible warning of what the crowd may do. Still, his revenge is provoked not by the preaching, but by the unnatural behaviour of his victim, Tito. What might be taken as evidence of the crowd's rationality—its political purposefulness—is converted to a matter of appetite, since the vote will serve as an anodyne to the working man's stomach. Popular agitation is naive, corrupt, even egoistic—like the ruling class which incites it. Yet the novel's portrayal of the Florentine situation makes the case for some kind of change, and Eliot cannot argue convincingly against Savonarola's entrance into politics, whose corrupting effect relies on authorial assertion. She fails to dramatise her heroine's alternative to political improvement.

In A Tale of Two Cities, Dickens' liberal sympathies cannot survive the imaginative recreation of the consequences of revolution. Romola, on the other hand, is consistently conservative. The oppressed do not move in the same world as the political oppressors, and the mob is powerless to surprise: "all things except reason and order are possible with a mob". Unlike Dickens, Eliot planned her dissolution of the social milieu towards the end of her novel, when Romola drifts to the plague-struck village and pursues her charitable functions in incorruptible isolation. She wrote to Sara Hennell in 1863 that "the 'Drifting away' and the Village with the Plague belonged to my earliest vision of the story and were by deliberate forecast adopted as romantic and symbolical elements". If Dickens' novel is a progressive self-revelation, Eliot's is the predictable consequence of a confirmed viewpoint.

There are not the forebodings of revolution in Eliot's letters that we find in Dickens'. She did not agree with him that English society was radically corrupt, or see reform as the one way of averting revolution. On the contrary, reform seemed the great danger. Chapter XXXV of *Romola*, "What Florence was Thinking of", relates to what England was thinking of in the years preceding the 1867 Reform Act:

> . . . was Florence to have a Great Council, after the Venetian mode, where all the officers of government might be elected, and all laws voted by a wide number of citizens of a certain age and of ascertainable qualifications, without question of rank or party? or, was it to be governed on a narrower and less popular scheme, in which the hereditary influence of good families would be less adulterated with the votes of shopkeepers?

Eliot shared the Conservative and Adullamite dread of a legislative revolution once the working class was in a voting majority, and the indiscriminate violence of the residuum which she warned against in "Felix Holt's Address" was a metaphor for parliamentary "violence". She had not been converted to Bagehot's faith in the deference of the masses by 1868, and in her novel of 1863, wished to affirm through her heroine that popular politics was not the only means to social improvement.

Auguste Comte, creator of the Positivist philosophy, blamed anarchy less on the ruled than the rulers, who were responsible for reconciling conflicting interests. He thought the workers highly endowed morally, if not mentally. The affective workers in society corresponded to the emotions in the individual, and were the natural allies under Positivism of the new Spiritual Power, the scientific priesthood, which was to channel working-class feeling. Together, they would humanise the employers' capitalism. On its banner, Positivism coupled progress with order; and for the English Positivists, like Eliot's friends Frederic Harrison and E. S. Beesly, order was no reactionary catchword, but the principle which justified their absorption in radical politics, since the anarchists were not the workers.

The attraction of Positivism for Eliot was that while politics were granted a limited usefulness in stabilising society as a condition for future progress, that was never conceived in political terms. The moral evolution of the species was the true progress, not to be hastened by political measures. Comte and Eliot agreed that the workers had no power to decide the ordering of society, though they might (Eliot is willing to allow in *Felix Holt*) help the Spiritual Power shape public opinion. This, "the greatest power under heaven," according to Holt, is "the ruling belief in society about what is right and what is wrong, what is honourable and what is shameful. That's the steam that is to work the engines". We may suspect that here, Eliot was conceding moral influence to the workers to divert them from politics: her distaste for the masses was more pronounced than Comte's. She was pessimistic about what might be expected from working-class nature, and in "The Natural History of German Life", criticised Dickens for perpetrating in his novels "the miserable fallacy, that high morality and refined sentiment can grow out of harsh social relations, ignorance, and want. . . ." There was no social contribution for the workers to make, except to submit quietly to higher guidance.

Eliot's presentation of Savonarola in *Romola* was related to Comte's writings on medieval Europe, and especially the institution of the Catholic Church. She read the *Philosophie Positive* (1830–42) while working on the novel, and was "thankful to learn" from the luminous survey of the Middle Ages. Through all obstacles, claimed Comte,

> . . . Catholicism fulfilled its great provisional office, giving to the world, by its mere existence, an example which will never be lost of the inestimable influence on the improvement of society of a genuine spiritual authority, such as we have need of now, and shall obtain, when we have ascertained an intellectual basis for it, more direct, broader, and more durable than that of Catholicism.[4]

According to Comte's "Loi des Trois Etats", there were three necessary stages in the evolution of opinion and society. For the

[4] I quote from Harriet Martineau's condensed translation, *The Positivist Philosophy of Auguste Comte*, 1853.

supernaturalism and ascriptions to providence of the Theological phase, the Metaphysical substituted a belief in abstract forces: politically, the divine right to rule was superseded by the natural right of the ruled to elect. The Positivist era, still in the future and impartially contemptuous of divinities and the resort to first principles, would study phenomena scientifically and provide for the new spiritual authority the true foundation that Catholicism lacked. In *Romola*, as G. A. Santangelo notes, while Savonarola regenerates the heroine, her final estrangement is caused by the narrowness of his moral prescriptions. She is repulsed by his dogmas and prophecies, and gradually finds inhuman and rejects the command that she shall return to her erring husband, Tito.

Battling against a corrupt society and Papacy, Savonarola's first concern is with the purification of public opinion. By Eliot's reckoning, he is the genuine social reformer preoccupied, like Felix Holt, not with the engines but the steam that drives the engines. But his visionary sensationalism induces a mixed audience, and the mob appreciates "the false certitude which gave his sermons the interest of a political bulletin": for his own sake and theirs, once the masses are aroused, the orator must retain mastery at the cost of principle. Savonarola succumbs to the "vitiating influence of party interests", when his advocacy of the Great Council was intended to counteract. Resorting to popular politics, he is entering the Metaphysical or Negative phase, which destroyed the false accretions and dogmas of Catholicism, but in a changed form perpetuated the old Theological vices. Romola is now repelled by his Metaphysical narrowness and addiction to political dogma. The reform which had once inspired her seemed "to reduce itself to narrow devices for the safety of Florence, in contemptible contradiction to the alternating professions of blind trust in the divine care". If an obsession with popular rights is a natural manifestation of the Metaphysical phase, under Positivism, "the vague and stormy discussion of *rights* will be replaced by the calm and precise determinations of duties". Comte takes it for granted that egoism is the essence of striving after ends by political means, and so does Eliot: Savonarola's growing egoism does not have to be demonstrated.

The implausibility of charging with political ambition the austere monk Savonarola, bent on the realisation of a sternly

Christian society, was accepted in Eliot's time. The *British Quarterly Review* remarked in 1849 that it was impossible to doubt the purity of Savonarola's motives, though the reformer was mistaken in imagining that wise and prosperous government might be achieved through legislative enactments. In 1857, the *Saturday Review* stated that there was "no need to ask any explantation of Savonarola's failure except in his ideas. They express mediaeval religion in its highest and purest form, but a form which was lifeless, because it did not belong to the society of the day". Eliot's main source for Savonarola's career, Villari's *Life and Times of Girolamo Savanarola* (1859–61), had more respect for the great liberator than to assign him to the dismal Middle Ages. Despite theological narrowness, his hallucinations and blunders, Savonarola emerged as an heroic Renaissance type, though superbly free from the egoism with which he is attributed by Eliot. She was attracted to Villari because his tendentious historical placing of the reformer gave leeway to her own modernisation. For Comte, the Metaphysical phase began with Protestantism, and Savonarola in *Romola* is no medieval throwback but an embryo-Protestant, combining with Theological vices those perpetuated in the nineteenth century. Generally, too, Villari's account of Savonarola chimed with her Positivist sympathies. While others were concerned only with intellectual renovation, Savonarola stood for the moral renovation of mankind, and won the admiration of the scholars whose excesses he combated, since the paganism of the Renaissance left a painful void in their souls. But like the Swiss historian Sismondi, whose *Histoire des Republiques Italiennes du Moyen Age* (1809–18) Eliot perused, Villari was a liberal, to whom the dawn of Comte's Metaphysical era was the birth of freedom. Eliot appreciated the liberal attack on the pagan tyranny of the Medici family, but could not enthuse over the popular opposition.

Consistently with Comte, Eliot differed from Villari in stressing the egoism bred by Savonarola's involvement in popular politics. The Savonarola of *Romola* is discredited over the issue of the right of appeal for the Medicean conspirators, bent on the restoration of Piero de Medici, Lorenzo's mediocre successor. Savonarola had himself advocated the Appeal from the Six Votes, but in Eliot's account, betrays his principles once they are a liability.

Allan Gilbert, in his introduction to *The Prince and other works*, points out that Eliot turned to Machiavelli's *Discourses* for her own interpretation of Savonarola's conduct; and in the novel, Machiavelli acts as her mouthpiece. According to the *Discourses*, Savonarola's failure to condemn the breach of the right of appeal "made it plain to all that at heart he was ambitious and a party-man": such was the view of the reformer's well-born enemies in Florence.

Savonarola's career is made exemplary of that of the popular orator in any age. Eliot read Bulwer's *Rienzi* (1835) in preparation for writing *Romola*, and much as she despised Bulwer as a novelist, drew the same moral from Savonarola's downfall as was extracted from Rienzi's. This, writes Bulwer,

> is the true misfortune of a man nobler than his age—that the instruments he must use soil himself: half he reforms his times; but half, too, the times will corrupt the reformer. His own craft undermines his safety;—the people, whom he himself accustoms to a false excitement, perpetually craves it; and when their ruler ceases to seduce their fancy, he falls their victim.

For the populace, the lesson is that "their own passions are the real despots they should subdue, their own reason the true regenerator of abuses". In 1856, H. H. Milman's essay on Savonarola in the *Quarterly Review* concluded: "Woe to him who excites the populace to the madness of high-wrought expectation, to be succeeded by the madness of disappointment." The issue of Eliot's painstaking research was a conventional response towards the mythical demagogue.

Eliot is proposing an option to politics as a remedy for social ills, and the heroine, Romola, is intended to show a better way through Positivism. Ahead of her age, she is dissatisfied with its theological-metaphysical extravagances. Comte wished to inspire in the reader of his *Philosophie Positive* the consoling conviction "that the most advanced of the human race are at the threshold of a social order worthy of their nature and their needs". It is generally remarked, however, that Romola satisfies her reforming impulse only when she drifts from Florence and the complexities besetting Savonarola. The villagers' problem is the plague, a natural calamity, rather than class-rule. Undeniably, Savonarola appears to be confronted in Florence with political problems. Eliot may argue that the correct solution is independent of politics, but she cannot make her case by facing her heroine with a situation bearing no analogy to Savonarola's. In the Prelude to *Middlemarch*, Eliot bewails the fate of latter-day St Theresas, "helped by no coherent social faith and order", and with "no epic life wherein there was a constant unfolding of far-resonant action". The epic life here is a sentimental abstraction, and the force of most of *Middlemarch* is to define it as such. Romola is a Dorothea Brooke whose aspirations are not thwarted by an observed environment, and the heroine of the Florentine novel is indulged with her slice of epic life. The lapse into blank verse betrays how the floating to the village and Positivist self-fulfilment is a retreat from history, and the new life is heavily associated with the death-wish. With Romola as an updated Madonna, a preliminary vision of the Positivist era joins the Theological and Metaphysical eras within the novel, but remains Eliot's mere "symbolical element".

Romola's isolation in the village reflects her loneliness throughout the novel. The precursor of the new era has been involved in the Florentine dissensions of her own age only at second hand. Eliot wrote to Sara Hennell that "the various *strands* of thought I had to work out forced me into a more ideal treatment of Romola than I had foreseen from the outset . . ."; and this was true. The sustaining of the novel's thesis depended on the heroine's idealisation, which was a characteristically Positivist habit of mind. Both Comte and Eliot often stressed that individuals were determined by their environment as much as they determined that environment. But Comte, who claimed to have made sociology a "positive" science, tended not to allow for the social conditioning of his own intellect, and to assume that Positivism might be realised by appealing to other intellects as autonomous as his own. Accomplished in one mind, a widespread regeneration was sooner or later secure. Romola's history, that of the making of a Positivist, relies on our taking for granted the broad social significance of the personal illumination.

There has been an inclination, among critics of *Romola*, to salvage Tito Melema as a typical creation of George Eliot, the supreme psychologist; though his appearance in Renaissance Florence suggests a mechanical element in the psychology. In accordance with the novel's strategy, Tito, as a psychological case, is insulated from an historical conditioning less decisive than it seems. Eliot was grateful to R. H. Hutton for perceiving "the relation of the Florentine political life to the development of Tito's nature", and there is a clear sense in which he shares the class-egoism of the patricians. We read in *The Stones of Venice* that scholars wore, instead of gowns, "a chain mail, whose purpose was not so much to avert the weapon of the adversary as to restrain the motions of the wearer", and Tito's career reflects Ruskin's metaphorical expressions of the Renaissance mentality. To ward off the vengeance of his stepfather, Tito buys a suit of chain-mail; and Eliot capitalises on the figurative possibilities of this "garment of fear". Tito's course is that of Ruskin's Venetians, who fell "from pride to infidelity, and from infidelity to the unscrupulous *pursuit of pleasure*".

Disconcertingly, though, Tito's is also the egoism of Everyman. Eliot writes of his impulsive renunciation of his stepfather that Tito experienced "that inexorable law of human souls, that we prepare ourselves for sudden deeds by the reiterated choice of good or evil that gradually determines character". The substitution of human for class psychology means that Tito can be isolated as abnormally wicked, and not really typical of his Renaissance environment. If the Florentine ruling class exhibits Titoesque egoism, it is to a lesser degree which makes a qualitative difference. Eliot is similarly evasive in creating Tito a Greek, an alien in Florence. There does not seem much to choose between Greek and Florentine egoism, and it is partly the point that there is not. But thanks to his status as the slippery Greek, Tito can never be quite representative of the Florentine patricians.

The psychological formulae governing the moral progress of Tito, and also Savonarola, seem to derive from Herbert Spencer's *Social Statics*, published in 1851. Spencer was a close friend, and both Eliot and Lewes particularly admired this book, which ascribed the sum of human misery to the process of adaptation from primitive individualism to the social state, a hypothetical entity where social altruism (or enlightened self-interest) prevailed. Since the state was "a mere dead mechanism worked by a nation's moral sense", no one would be socialised the faster through legislative enactments. The whole burden of adaptation fell on the individual, and success depended on the avoidance of what Spencer termed the "practical atheism" of moral pragmatism. Rather than deciding for ourselves what will be good or bad for mankind,

> we are to search out with a genuine humility the rules ordained for us – are to do unfalteringly, without speculating as to consequences, whatsoever these require; and we are to do this in the belief that then, when there is perfect sincerity – when each man is true to himself—when every one strives to realize what he thinks the highest rectitude—then must all things prosper.

Spencer's class-bias is reflected in his low evolutionary rating of the masses, less moral and therefore less human than their social superiors. When Eliot wrote in *Romola* of "the vaguely active animal spirits" of the carnival crowd, she used "animal" precisely. Spencer thought the degradation of the masses a consequence of their conditioning, and was impatient with those who railed against the mob and ignored the conditions. In *Romola* and *Felix Holt*, the animus latent in both Spencer's and Comte's placid dehumanisation of the masses is very evident. By the time of *Middlemarch*, the reform issue had ceased to worry Eliot, and she treated the lower orders with more equanimity.

Tito and Savonarola are condemned in their respective departures from the laws of the social state. Tito moves steadily further from the highest rectitude ("what motive could any man really have, except his own interest"), and Savonarola shows a blind willingness to let ends justify means. Their lurid deaths—Tito's murder by Baldassare, Savonarola's burning—are, on one level, appropriate punishments for moral turpitude. Spencer remarks grimly that there are no reprieves for the disobedient. Like the masses and his contadina, Tessa (more bird or fish than human), but without their excuse, Tito is full of animal propensities: "a timid animal urged to a desperate leap by the terror of the tooth and the claw that are close behind it". Unable to adapt to his own more sophisticated conditions of existence, Tito suffers social expulsion. Though reappropriated by sociologists unaware of their debt, "the survival of the fittest" was Spencer's phrase before it was Darwin's. Savonarola, too, succumbs to the utilitarian pragmatism especially characteristic of politicians, whose attempts to interpose between humanity and the conditions of existence only retard the process of adaptation. "Monetary panics, South-sea bubbles, Railway

116

manias, Irish rebellions, French revolutions,—these, and the miseries flowing from them, are but the cumulative effects of dishonesty," writes Spencer. "A bitter experience teaches all men when it is too late, that alike in national and individual affairs, entire submission is the wisest course." While distributing the weight of misery which is mankind's until character adapts to meet the conditions of the social state, all government is immoral in employing "evil weapons to subjugate evil". Savonarola's fall from grace is like that of the Middlemarch banker, Bulstrode, who differentiates God's cause from his own rectitude of conduct and feels free to use God's enemies instrumentally. But while in *Middlemarch*, moral determinism coexists with an acute analysis of the Nonconformist conscience, Savonarola's career is the mere Spencerian parable.

The doctrinal sources of *Romola* were multifarious, and Eliot herself was an acknowledged influence on Spencer. But clearly, Eliot had authority for treating the Renaissance as analogous with her own time. Writing on Venice, Ruskin saw moral emotions, rather than specific events and conditions, as the true history, and the emotions were also the history of the nineteenth century. More deliberately, since social progress was considered one with the evolution of individuals, Spencer and Comte subordinated events to emotions, and attributed historical significance to the individual moral life. So did Eliot in the novel, and as her age was still striving, like Florence in the fifteenth century, towards Positivism or the social state, *Romola* was equipped with the modern moral truth which Lewes had insisted that historical fiction should purvey. A strong candidate for the new Savonarola was Mazzini, the Italian republican. It is Eliot's point that the Florentine allegory might be cast with contemporary personae: Savonarola and Mazzini, however, attracted and repelled her in similar ways.

Italian historiography scanned the past for precursors of the struggle for national identity, and naturally associated the Risorgimento with the Renaissance. In his defiance of the papacy, Savonarola was well qualified for the role of nationalist before his time. Villari's great purpose was to prove Savonarola's name "one of the most glorious on Italy's noble list of thinkers, heroes and martyrs", and so to inspire his own generation. For Eliot, too, Savonarola deserved resurrection, but ultimately as warning rather than example. The utility of the Spiritual Power in Positivist society depended on its observance of the distinction between theory and practice. In Mazzini's case as well as Savonarola's, Eliot admired the theory and condemned the practice.

Enthusing over the February revolution of 1848, Eliot compared the English working class unfavourably with "the mass of the French people". "Here there is so much larger a proportion of selfish radicalism and an unsatisfied, brute sensuality . . . than of perception or desire of justice, that a revolutionary movement would be simply destructive—not constructive." The urban artisans in England, Eliot seems to have felt, were unduly preoccupied with narrow class interests; and she was making the same criticism of Savonarola in accusing him of egoism. The view that moral emotions superior to economics should inspire the reformer, and the tendency to confound philosophical and vulgar definitions of materialism, were shared by Mazzini. In an essay of 1870, "From the Council to God", he equated the materialism which he associated with the theories of the French socialists with "the exclusive worship of material well-being" that he blamed for extinguishing Italian liberties in the sixteenth century. Like Savonarola, Mazzini proclaimed his revolt against an era of barren individualism. His creed was congenial to the mind that learned from Comte, and in her account of the fortunes of the Florentine republic, Eliot realised Mazzini's vision of "the darkness of a world deprived of all ideal", where "in a brief tormented existence, ungoverned by any law save sensation and the appetites to which it gives rise, the answer of mankind to every moral lesson will be, *Egotism*".

While sympathising with Mazzini, the social philosopher, Eliot was wary of the man of action, the conspirator; though Mazzini remarked that the choice was not his, and that the authorities never allowed him to practise his philosophical apostate in peace. Eliot refused in 1865 to subscribe to a fund for Mazzini, since the Florentine committee was vague about the precise application, and the money might be used to promote conspiracy.

> Now, though I believe there are cases in which conspiracy may be a sacred, necessary struggle against organised wrong, there are also cases in which it is hopeless, and can produce nothing but misery; or needless, because it is not the best means attainable of reaching the desired end; or unjustifiable, because it resorts to

acts which are more unsocial in their character than the very wrong they are directed to extinguish: and in these three supposable cases it seems to me that it would be a social crime to further conspiracy even by the impulse of a little finger, to which one may well compare a small money contribution.

Eliot discusses here the problem facing both Savonarola and Romola, where sacred obedience ends and sacred rebellion begins. Savonarola is right to resist the Pope, and Romola, in her turn, to resist Savonarola; but social defiance is a different matter. Despite Eliot's concession, it would be hard to imagine an actual conspiracy which she could conscientiously support. She wrote in "Felix Holt's Address" that resistance to oppression was probably useless, because collectively men would always be narrow and greedy rather than farsighted and generous. Only the gullible will share the democratic aspirations of Renaissance Florentines, Mazzini's adherents, or the English workers of 1868.

Romola's modern moral pervaded contemporary English novels dealing with Mazzini's part in the Risorgimento. In Amelia Blandford Edwards' *Half a Million of Money*, published in 1865, the revolutionary conspirator Guilio Colonna is a portrait of Mazzini. He is criticised in Spencerian terms: evidence rather of the relation of *Social Statics* to the middle-class orthodoxy than any direct indebtedness. Colonna is "a great man, a noble man, an heroic man, after his kind", but "wholly dominated by a single idea, and unable to recognise any but his own arbitrary standard of right and wrong". It is the characteristic fault of *Romola* that Eliot, like Miss Edwards or Bulwer in *Rienzi*, feels free to abstract the enthusiast from history. The historical novels of the 1850s and 1860s tended to regress to the platitudes of the Enlightenment which Carlyle, in 1830, had hoped were verging towards extinction, "even in England where they linger the latest". But by the 1860s, the moralising habit indicated less confidence that history was an open book for all to read, than an incapacity and unwillingness to recover its secrets. Conventional attitudes were under challenge in *Romola* more than in the works of minor novelists like Miss Edwards: the debate between Romola and Savonarola is left finely poised, and Eliot remarks correctively that "tender fellow-feeling for the nearest has its dangers too", as her heroine scolds the reformer for sacrificing means to ends. Perhaps Eliot's gener-

119

osity to Savonarola at the close reflected her sense of the irrelevance of the charge against him.

In her essay of 1856, "The Antigone and its Moral", Eliot makes the moral a key to historical interpretation:

> resist the payment of ship-money, you bring on civil war; preach against false doctrines, you disturb feeble minds and send them adrift on a sea of doubt; . . . Wherever the strength of a man's intellect, or moral sense, or affection brings him into opposition with the rules which society has sanctioned, *there* is renewed the conflict between Antigone and Creon. . . .

Eliot modernises Antigone and Creon as naturally as she does the seventeenth-century St Theresa of the Prelude to *Middlemarch*, or Savonarola and the heroine (a pet-name is Antigone) in *Romola*. The dilemma is in the mind of the nineteenth-century beholder, denying historical process and trying to persuade her contemporaries to abstention: there is "no right thread to pull". *Romola* cannot be praised for refusing to simplify large moral questions, when the questions are anachronistic and abstract. But it is to George Eliot's credit that she is less willing than other novelists of the age to play the severe schoolmarm. Rather than lecturing the more progressive of history's great men on their immorality, she merely begs them to consider what they do.

"Felix Holt the Radical"

The Introduction to *Felix Holt the Radical*, set in the 1830s in England, is an impressive attempt to confront the problems of industrialism, and while country and town are sharply contrasted as the stage-coach traverses Loamshire, Eliot refrains from idyllising the country. There is nothing idyllic about her description of the hamlets of labourers' cottages with "their little dingy windows telling, like thick-filmed eyes, of nothing but the darkness within", and Eliot is directing attention beyond the circumscribed view of the detached passenger on the box-seat who, "bowled along above such a hamlet, saw chiefly the roofs of it". Writing of the men with considerable banking accounts who remarked that "they never meddled with politics themselves", Eliot is not identified with them. They can afford the pretence of abstention, not because they rule an idyllic countryside, but because working conditions in the country preclude a concerted challenge to their authority. Only in the towns has the concentration of labour in mines and factories created the consciousness of an identity of interests which was a necessary prelude to class struggle.

Even in the Introduction, however, there is an urge to idealise which gathers strength as the novel proceeds. Eliot describes the cottages of the country labourers, not their consciousnesses; but when she enters into that of the shepherd, it is reasonable to ask (as Raymond Williams does in *The Country and the City*, where he sees nostalgia for rural life as dominating the Introduction) how she knows that the shepherd "felt no bitterness except in the matter of pauper labourers and the bad-luck that sent contrarious seasons and the sheep-rot". Significantly, the shepherd is caught where he works and not, like the labourers, where he lives; and his walk is "timed by the walk of grazing beasts". Perhaps, then, there is agitation in the town and not in the country because there the workers are content. The urban workers' inner life cannot be stylised, and its direct contemplation merely repulses the author. Her hero withdraws from the antagonisms of Treby, moving to an urban environment, admittedly, but one which is carefully undefined: "as to the town in which Felix Holt now resides, I will keep that a secret. . . ." The hope of retiring from contradiction and conflict to more peaceful climes remains intact.

As Felix Holt is in the anomalous position of being the only craftsman in North Loamshire, and free from the social pressures afflicting the Sproxton miners, his insistence on his allegiance to his class cannot count for much in the novel. Only by token does Eliot reject the middle-class panacea that workers should themselves become capitalists; but she is still making a point of some interest in her early treatment of Holt. His education—a medical apprenticeship—is bought with the proceeds from his father's patent medicines, so that accident gives Holt the option of rising socially. *Felix Holt* is much concerned with education of one kind and another. One kind the workers are expected to acquire, and the other costs money. Holt's money comes from a dubious source, and in the social context of the oppressed masses depicted in the Introduction, the honesty of the money enabling Mrs Transome to sneer at Wordsworth and Esther Lyon to dote on Byronic heroes is put into question. At this stage in the novel, Eliot is not

121

far from the Meredithian view as stated in *Sandra Belloni*: "those 'fine feelers', or antennae of the senses, come of sweet ease; that is synonymous with gold in our island latitude".

The society portrayed in the Introduction to *Felix Holt* is in the throes of the Industrial Revolution. The ruling class is itself threatened by the forces which an advanced capitalism has brought into being, and vainly attempts to shelter behind "fine old woods . . . allowing only peeps at the park and mansion which they shut in from the working-day world". In *The Stones of Venice*, Ruskin had condemned the aristocracies which gathered themselves into festering isolation and provoked the French Revolution; and the Renaissance poison of a class-divided society was still operative in the nineteenth century and in England. Never, Ruskin wrote in his chapter on "The Nature of Gothic",

> had the upper classes so much sympathy with the lower, or charity for them, as they have at this day, and yet never were they so much hated by them: for, of old, the separation between the noble and the poor was merely a wall built by law; now it is a veritable difference in level of standing, a precipice between upper and lower grounds in the field of humanity, and there is pestilential air at the bottom of it.

The art of the Renaissance, according to Ruskin, was typically that of an aristocratic coterie, rigidly inhuman and unable to concede to the populace. Similarly, the paintings at Transome Court, which Esther Lyon is in danger of inheriting and where Mrs Transome is trapped, are seen as reflecting the intransigencies of a class. Having learnt of her legal title, Esther stays at the mansion and complains to her host, Harold Transome, that nearly all the portraits are "in a conscious, affected attitude. That fair Lady Betty looks as if she had been drilled into that posture, and had not will enough of her own ever to move again". After a visit in 1855 to the Paris Exposition of English Art, Dickens remarked of the paintings on view that there was "a horrid respectability about most of the best of them—a little, finite, systematic routine in them, strangely expressive to me of the state of England itself". Making the connection herself in *Felix Holt*, Eliot is conveying not the private world of the Transomes but a social condition.

We read in *The Stones of Venice* that the Venetian ruling class was exclusively concerned with its own physical pleasure, and decorated walls and roofs with a pagan lasciviousness. Such licence seems at odds with Lady Betty's horrid respectibility, but there is no contradiction in her finding herself in the company of pagan gods at Transome Court: Mrs Transome is both respectable and lascivious, like Ruskin's Venetians, whose moral corruption was the price of their class-consciousness. Appropriately, then, the house abounds in Greek statuary: there is Apollo, and Silenus carrying the infant Bacchus. Mrs Holt visits Transome Court to instigate an appeal on her son's behalf against the sentence incurred by his part in the Treby election riot, and in the hallway, mistakes the naked figure of Silenus for an eccentric ancestral Transome. This is a humorous reflection of Ruskin's point about the class-bound nature of Renaissance art, whose excellences were all the product of deep erudition, and the kind that "no common mind can taste".

Bred to believe that society exists for their own pleasure, the inhabitants of Transome Court invite nemesis as surely as Ruskin's Venetians. Eliot's brief biography of the elder brother Durfey, gambler and imbecile, is a melodramatic outline of the moral fall attending his half-brother Harold, his mother Mrs Transome, and her former lover and Harold's father, the solicitor Jermyn. The faithless Mrs Transome abandons herself to the pursuit of pleasure and an affair with the young Jermyn. But the child of the union is also an egoist, without time for the delicacies of filial consideration, and Harold's mother is punished for her sin. Ruskin blamed the scholars of the Renaissance for reducing men's thoughts and deeds to "so many different forms of fetter-dance"; and Harold Transome, himself imprisoned in class-egoism, threatens others' freedom. He had, we are told, "a padded yoke ready for the neck of every man, woman and child that depended on him", and to Esther Lyon, life at Transome Court was "a silken bondage that arrested all motive". As opposed to Harold and his dangerous comforts, it is broadly hinted that Felix Holt is a pre-Renaissance figure. He "might have come from the hands of a sculptor in the later Roman period, when the plastic impulse was stirred by the grandeur of barbaric forms"; and still less equivocally, he has a "great Gothic head". One way of explaining Holt's isolation as the only crafts-man in North Loamshire is to see him as Ruskin's ideal workman already realised, using his head as well as his hands in a society

otherwise split between "morbid thinkers, and miserable workers".
But Holt is as much estranged from the Sproxton miners as if he
had practised medicine, while the labour slaves, whose fate Ruskin
wished to alleviate, remain condemned to the degrading work
which makes them less than men. Eliot was never hopeful that the
masses could be found satisfying employment, and Ruskin's social
ethic is caricatured. There is more prevarication in her treatment
of Esther Lyon, very like the young ladies censured by Ruskin in
"The Nature of Gothic", where they are asked to consider the consequences of their indulgence. The fashion for glass beads, and
pins whose points were polished with "sand of the human soul",
doomed myriads of workers to a terrible monotony; and at the
Treby hustings, the trade-unionist tells the crowd that "it isn't a
man's share just to mind your pin-making, or your glass-blowing".
On Holt's first meeting with Esther, Eliot remarks that to her
hero, "a fine lady was always a sort of spun-glass affair—not
natural, and with no beauty for him as art". Servitude corrupts
the slaves less than the slavemasters, and the young ladies are
as stereotyped as the glass beads they wear.

Esther, with her petty desires, represents for a future husband
the trap that she herself avoids in rejecting Transome Court;
until she is revivified by Holt. The 'spun-glass" element is
banished, and she develops the individuality to which the workers,
one free from the tyranny of machine-made ornament, can also
aspire. Eliot comments of Esther's plea for Holt at his trial: "this
bright, delicate, beautiful-shaped thing that seemed most like a
toy or ornament—some hand had touched the chords, and there
came forth music that brought tears". Esther has learnt the Ruskinian lesson that there is no place for egoism in a society whose
masses are tainted and miserable. This sounds neat enough, but the
echoes of Ruskin jar with the developing plot. Ruskin's clinging to
the hope of a ruling-class change of heart is incongruous in "The
Nature of Gothic", which shows the force of social conditioning.
It is also a recurrent piety in mid-Victorian investigations of the
working-class problem. But while in Ruskin the means remain
nebulous, there is no doubt as to the end in view. What must proceed from the change of heart is not mere goodwill among classes,
but a peaceful revolution in the economic structure of society.
There is reason for the ruling class to feel guilty, and reason for it

to act. Oddly, *Felix Holt* does not leave us with any such feeling; and even the appeal to paternalism, which we find in Gaskell's *Mary Barton* and *North and South*, is absent here. Finally, it is more than Eliot can admit that there is cause for the ruling class to feel even guilty, and Holt the "social reformer"—the *Edinburgh Review* thought this title more appropriate than "Radical"—is free to leave Treby altogether, whither we are not told. There is no suggestion that he will preach in "some large town . . . some ugly, wicked miserable place", his earlier motive for predicting his departure from Treby.

Esther's rejection of luxury at Transome Court is socially irrelevant, since it is prompted less by enlightened self-interest—Ruskin thinks that there will be a revolution if the ruling class does not behave better—than her immediate advantage. Esther envisages life at the house not in terms of the moral dangers besetting fine ladies, but in those of the loneliness traditionally afflicting the poor little rich girl. Of course, Eliot has presented mansions sheltering from the workaday world as necessarily lonely places. But Esther's objection is less to the role than its unfamiliarity. Her hopeless vagueness about what to do with her wealth, in a novel stressing the poverty of the masses, suggests that she has not absorbed her Ruskinian lesson very thoroughly. The credibility of Holt's radicalism diminishes with the demand: set in the private world of parable, Transome Court has nothing to teach Esther about class.

Despite his insights into the mid-Victorian economy, Ruskin was too nervous of the workers whom he was sometimes accused of inciting to see them as a force for change which society had generated. The ruling classes had to be persuaded to altruism. Eliot did not turn from Ruskin in *Felix Holt* simply through being unable to contemplate peaceful revolution with his equanimity. While she was glad to follow his lead in relating social disharmony to egoism, she did not see as an historical occurrence the rise of the bourgeois sensibility, and could not conceive of its transformation. Consequently, she was less Utopian than Ruskin, but without an alternative to the change of heart, all she could do was to make moral reform and her reformer superfluous by dissipating the social evils which were the novel's theme.

Far from wishing to medievalise industrial society, as the ortho-

125

dox Gothic revivalists tended to do, Ruskin hoped that a revolution in values would lead to a genuinely contemporary adaptation of Gothic. But while he was writing, Joseph Paxton had assumed the role of the medieval architect, and was expressing in the most appropriate materials social values which were resistant to transformation. George Eliot gives her hero his Gothic head, though her allusion to the past is at odds with her scepticism about changes of heart. In *Great Expectations*, Dickens is a consistent critic of Ruskin. Wemmick, who alternates between the contemporary world of work, and Gothic leisure, is not what Ruskin hoped to make of humanity; and to that extent, Dickens seems to be censuring the orthodox revivalists and not Ruskin. On the other hand, echoes of "The Nature of Gothic" are unmistakable, and there was no confusion in Dickens' mind. The conditioning power of the modern city ruled out a spontaneous change of heart. Despite his preoccupation with his own age, Ruskin's version of the nature of Gothic is suggested to be as irrelevant as any other to the nineteenth century.

Wemmick is as Gothic as Felix Holt, but the revival at Walworth is coyly escapist. The house is the smallest that Pip had ever seen: "with the queerest gothic windows (by far the greater part of them sham), and a gothic door, almost too small to get in at". There is none of that great social evil denounced by Ruskin, the division of labour, at Walworth, and Wemmick proudly informs Pip, "I am my own engineer, and my own carpenter, and my own plumber, and my own Jack of all Trades. . . ." But the achieved ideal at home is notable for its pathetic variance with his work in London, where as clerk to the solicitor Jaggers, he acts out his employer's inhumanity. He is not free to choose; and leaving for the city, looks as unconscious of the Gothic paraphernalia as if it had all been blown into space by his cannon, the Stinger.

More briefly, and in a lighter vein, Wilkie Collins is attacking the orthodox revivalist rather than Ruskin in *The Woman in White*, where the gentry of Welmingham, anxious to restore the medieval church in the old town, issue prospectuses flourished with Gothic devices and appealing for funds. Despite the devices, money is not forthcoming—"what *can* you expect out of London?", asks the church clerk—and the church becomes increasingly dilapidated, until it is burnt down by Sir Percival Glyde. To Ruskin, restoration meant "the most total destruction which a building can suffer". It was impossible, he wrote "as impossible as to raise the dead, to restore anything that has ever been great or beautiful in architecture". In the last decade of the nineteenth century, Hardy in *Jude the Obscure* (1895) portrayed the crumbling Gothic of Christminster, the university city whose dons defend a bankrupt past against the advances of men like Jude. The stonemason and aspiring student finds work renovating the lichened colleges; not a pursuit which Ruskin would have approved, but he is reasonably included in Hardy's indictment. Jude is slow to appreciate "that mediaevalism was as dead as a fern-leaf in a lump of coal; that other developments were shaping in the world around him, in which Gothic architecture and its associations had no place".

In his brilliant essay on *Felix Holt*, Arnold Kettle argues that Eliot's passive acceptance of the law, which dominates the plot, is at odds with the early criticism of the law-making society. But Eliot did not turn for information to her friend Frederic Harrison, the novel's legal adviser, in a merely neutral spirit. In the Introduction, the coachman observes of the conflicting claims to the Transome estate that "property didn't always get into the right hands"; and later, the solicitor Jermyn warns the wretched Tommy Trounsem, whose precarious existence secures the Transome possession, that if he meddles with the law, he will be caught "in a big wheel, and fly to bits". The law safeguards the rich, who can afford its deliberations, not the poor; and Jermyn's corruption is intimately related to his pursuit of the law, "a profession where much that is noxious may be done without disgrace". As much as Wilkie Collins in *The Woman in White*, Eliot seems to be preoccupied with the law as the most clearcut revelation of ruling-class values.

Still, this sceptical view of the law cannot be detected in the closing chapters. Despite Holt's low opinion of the justice generally dispensed in courts, his conviction for manslaughter, following the attempt to prevent mob violence at the Treby election, is recorded without irony. Instead of exemplifying class justice, it derives from "the rigid necessities of legal procedure". The law's actual bias is exposed when an appeal backed by the local gentry allows Holt to escape scot free; though as Arnold Kettle notes, Mrs Holt has been satirised precisely for supposing that the upper class could free her son if it felt inclined.

127

Herbert Spencer's *Social Statics* contains sweeping criticism of the law, especially property-law: the names of officers of the law, he writes, are "used as synonymes for trickery and greediness", and "the decisions of its courts are typical of chance". Spencer condemns prolonged chancery suits over inheritance, wasting the fortune of the contestants. More enigmatically, though, he shares the radical mistrust of legal procedure shown by Felix Holt, who is averse to a profession which defends the wicked for profit and imputes guilt to the virtuous. "The attempt to make a known felon appear innocent," comments Spencer, "denotes rather confused ideas of right and wrong." While Spencer is ready to concede that the age deserves a better legal system, he is not demanding legal reform. On the contrary, the crux of his argument is that the law inevitably reflects the vices of the age, which is why it cannot contribute to social improvement. Opposed to the law of the land was the absolute "moral law": men must stop judging what seems best and do what is abstractedly right. If we conformed to the moral law, if we were not selfish, legislative restraint would be unnecessary and government would not exist; and the unhappy corollary is that since we are selfish, legislators will make selfish laws, sacrificing the public good to their own benefit. When Eliot assails the law in *Felix Holt*, like Spencer she does so only to suggest the vanity of all legislation aiming to lessen the sum of human misery by mechanical means, and again the true standard is the moral law, as constant and universal as any physical law. Felix Holt knows that "the only failure a man ought to fear is failure in cleaving to the purposes he sees to be best"; and to Esther Lyon, "seemed to bring at once a law, and the love that gave strength to obey the law".

Felix Holt is always partly committed to the world of parable, with characters corrupt not only through class-nurture (that is one explanation), but also through their practical atheism in not holding fast to what they recognise as best. Harold Transome's actions are ruled by an utilitarian calculation of ends and means, and to Holt's rage, he is unwilling to condemn outright the practice of bribing the workers with beer, since their presence at the hustings can further his election to Parliament. But ends are incalculable, and the drink provokes the riot without helping to win the election. Harold Transome, in particular, and politicians generally (and Jermyn and lawyers generally) must learn that adherence to the moral law is the only salvation.

Spencer blamed the rudimentary morals of workers on their environment, but fear of the masses debarred Eliot from always making the connection, and caused her, towards the end of *Felix Holt*, to cease to view the law with Spencerian scepticism. As an emblem of human presumption, the law is excoriated and accused of bias, but Eliot moderates her tone in the particular instance when the law is a defence against popular disorder. Her hero's conviction and the circumstances of his successful appeal are merely recorded. Where once she had followed Spencer in arguing from a corrupt society to a corrupt judicature, now she remarks that everyone, including the judge, will see things from a personal point of view: "even the bare discernment of facts . . . must carry a bias". More than Spencer, she tended to regard the sub-humanity of the masses as a fixed condition, and it is clear here how her disparagement of politics was less the advocacy of true progress than the rationalisation of her fear of progress.

The candidate who wins the North Loamshire election is Philip Debarry, and Eliot is reasonably happy with the Conservative's victory. In 1873, when Gladstone's resignation had precipitated a ministerial crisis, she wrote to her publisher, John Blackwood, that she wished "there were some solid philosophical Conservative to take the reins—one who knows the true functions of stability in human affairs"; and in 1874, she did not "mind about the Conservative majority". Debarry, the philosophical conservative whom Eliot sought in the seventies, is scrupulous in his personal relations, treats his servants with deference, and dies a Catholic convert. We might sense irony in the reference to his conversion. The abortive debate between Rufus Lyon and the Church of England curate is an indication of theology's irrelevance to the questions posed by industrial society. But if Debarry's theology is retrograde, Eliot is very willing to dissipate contemporary pressures. English Positivists, like Harrison and Beesly, held that the true conservatism was radicalism, since the monied classes were the destructive element in society. Without her friends' confidence in the awakening masses, Eliot maintains that the best radicalism is the best kind of conservatism. In line with Comte's critique of the Catholic Church, Felix Holt offers a stronger intellectual basis for the Spiritual Power in society than a theological conservatism can provide. He refuses to attend church; similarly, there is no illumination for Esther in her father's "theory of providential arrangement". But the odd suggestion that Holt, and finally Esther, have more to advance than a cautious paternalism is never developed. Following Debarry's victory, the Positivists *in partibus* leave Treby, apparently satisfied that the unfaithful are well cared for.

Eliot's regression is associated with her fear of the workers who, in the 1860s, were agitating for reform. There is sympathy with them in the 1830s only so long as the "powerful men walking queerly with knees bent outwards" are seen in a generalised way, while a closer approach leads to the wish-fulfilment of the conclusion, where their existence is annulled. The *Pall Mall Gazette* commented, in July 1866, that

> the wealthy pay little heed to the change which is taking place in the habits of thought of the million; but when they read of strike after strike for increased wages, of prolonged conflicts between masters and men, and of the enormous development of the trades-union system, they begin to inquire about their own security, and almost to wish for a return to the blessed days when squires knew little, and shopkeepers knew less, and working people knew nothing at all.

Eliot's nervous insistence that popular education should precede reform of the franchise reflects her misgivings that the people are already too well instructed. In the "Address", Felix Holt's plea that the workers should educate their children ("here, it seems to me, is a way in which we may use extended co-operation among us to the most momentous of all purposes") is transparently a device to distract the unions from politics; and in the novel, the educational argument—it is finally the workers who must be enlightened, and not the ruling class, as in Ruskin—is also diversionary.

It is not clear what result Holt foresees should a popular franchise be conceded. At the beginning of his speech at the Treby hustings, he seems to be thinking in conventional terms of a "tyranny of the majority". Ignorant numbers have the power "to waste and destroy, to be cruel to the weak, to lie and quarrel, and to talk poisonous nonsense", so that to extend the franchise would make an immense difference, if only for the worse. But for the rest of his speech, Holt's contention is that while the moral degradation of the working class is prolonged, corrupt agents, like Johnson in the novel, will continue to place the same members in Parliament. The argument that the working-class vote might be nullified as a political force was respectable. The *Pall Mall Gazette*, in 1865, was amused by the rapturous reception and invitation to represent them in Parliament that the aristocratic Lord Amberley had from "the terrible working men of the North,— the hard-headed and horny-handed millions who have figured in so many novels as a kind of chorus of avengers". If the *Pall Mall* underestimated Amberley's radicalism, it was correct in supposing that the whole social fabric of the country would have to be transformed, before England became a democracy in the sense that France and America were democracies. While believing that a great *moral* change had been effected by the transposition of the legal balance of power from the wages-paying to the wages-earning class, Frederic Harrison wrote in the *Fortnightly Review* in 1868 that

> the corrupt boroughs, the bribery system, the nominee system, the jobbery system will perish hardly and slowly. Rank will exact its time-honoured spell, petty interests will divide constituencies as of old, and Beer will be king time and again.

But if Eliot and Felix Holt really believe in the nullification thesis, it is hard to account for the novel's polemical tone. As in the "Address", Eliot is afraid that the workers will have power and know how to use it; and the derision of that power as imaginary is purely tactical. The fall of the Hyde Park railings induced fear for property generally, and in the novel, the casual violence of the Treby riot suggests the legislative violence—class-legislation by the wrong class—that may be expected from the workers' admission to the franchise. In 1866, the *Pall Mall Gazette* reported that while Bright might be motivated by loathing for a supercilious aristocracy, his followers were intent on socialism. Universal suffrage was desired "as a class-weapon, a means of controlling legislation, according to the supposed interest of the more numerous classes".

Since socialism was assumed to be the aim of the reformers,

their unionist leadership created no surprise. In the 1860s, it was especially the development of trade-unionism which made the middle class fearful of mass-gatherings of the workers: processions, meetings, demonstrations, and anything that might be construed as riot. The speaker preceding Holt at the hustings, and provoking his denunciation of the demand for the franchise, is a unionist; and Eliot is too intelligent to portray him as the demagogue of middle-class myth. He is genuinely a working man, whereas according to Thomas Wright, the Journeyman Engineer, a characteristic of the professional agitator was his "fixed resolution never to do any hard work". The unionist is allowed to put forward his Chartist programme and, despite mistrusting Liberal aristocrats, to advise the workers to use their influence on Transome's behalf. He is then challenged by Holt, whose "look of habitual meditative abstraction from objects of mere personal vanity or desire, which is the peculiar stamp of culture", is distinguished from the previous speaker's "mere acuteness and rather hard-lipped antagonism". Man's primitive circumstances, according to Herbert Spencer, required that he should sacrifice others' welfare to his own, while his present circumstances require that he should not; so that the unionist's antagonism marks his unfitness for the social state. More immediately, it is the class antagonism which the middle class took to be the inspiration of the unionist movement. Increasingly in the novel, culture's mission is to deprecate antagonism as such, rather than the social conditions arousing class-consciousness; though Holt's fortuitous education has been a reminder that these conditions preclude the acquiring of culture by the masses, and Eliot has anyway viewed the process sceptically. That gold breeds its own values is borne out in Holt's case as well as Esther's and Mrs Transome's, though his *embourgeoisement* is unrecognised.

Matthew Arnold would rather write of the populace doing what it likes, but class antagonism composes the popular anarchy in *Culture and Anarchy*, and culture's hallmark is a contempt of politics. Arnold insists, of course, on culture's responsible awareness "that the sweetness and light of the few must be imperfect until the raw and unkindled masses of humanity are touched with sweetness and light"; but the means (or machinery) by which the millenium is to be realised are no more defined by Arnold than in the novel, and all is to be left to the individual cultured crusader, like Felix Holt. In Spencerian vein, Arnold's populace embraced the vices—ignorance, brutality, envy—vestigially present in aristo-cratic barbarian and middle-class philistine; and as these should subdue their baser nature, so in society must the workers be re-strained by the rationality of their superiors. Arnold's sweetness and light failed him in the face of the Hyde Park roughs, and Eliot is no gentler with the rioters at the Treby election. She congratu-lated Frederic Harrison on a witty parody of Arnold, and since she was as liable to stress the influence of environment on char-acter as that of character on environment, she was generally closer to her friend's position than Arnold's. But intent on decrying a resort to politics, she endowed her hero with persuasive powers overriding social conditioning.

Like her hero from the pages of *Blackwoods* in 1868, Eliot was preaching to the converted. For most of the reviewers of *Felix Holt*, that the radical of the title should turn out to be a con-servative was a blessing to be accepted, and how far his emergence in the true colours was an appropriate resolution to issues raised in the novel was not discussed. Increasingly, the urban poor were feared as an alien race. On a visit to Leeds in 1868, Eliot identified herself with the hearsay that the town's work people were "sadly coarse, beer-soaked bodies, with pleasures, mostly of the brutal sort, and the mill-girls 'epicene' creatures that make one shudder". It is in the context of such remarks that the force of Gladstone's mild insistence that the workers shared the "flesh and blood" of the other classes should be understood; and the shuddering recoil from the masses led to highly subjective interpretations of the past. Eliot was curiously distanced from her setting in the 1830s, and worked through the back files of *The Times* and *Annual Register* as though she were writing another *Romola*. Her research notes show that so far from giving substance and depth to a felt sense of the period, she approached the 1830s as a student, and was often surprised by the discoveries she made. Her difficulty in relating to the immediate past was rationalised in *Felix Holt* by dehistoricising the epoch of the first Reform Act.

There was an alarmed response in England to "scientific" history and particularly H. T. Buckle's *History of Civilization in England*, which was published in two volumes in 1857 and 1861. The decrying of Buckle's determinism was evoked by what seemed a controlling factor, the advance of democracy. Differing implications may attach to the claim that history is, or should be, scientific. The German historian, Leopold von Ranke, had urged that the evidence should be scrupulously amassed and analysed. Following Comte, Buckle wished to apply to historical writing the methodology of the natural sciences. As these proceeded by establishing general laws with which their phenomena complied, so he would define the laws of human development. In this sense, scientific history was partly a reaction against those of Ranke's disciples who, interpreting the master too dogmatically, thought that the historian's only charge was to relate what happened. Buckle objected to their interlarding of facts with armchair philosophising, but his own broad insistence that history was made by the ruled rather than the rulers was welcomed and abused as radicalism. Addressing the Birmingham and Midland Institute in 1870, Dickens made an unsatisfactory attempt to elucidate what he had meant, in his speech to the Institute the previous autumn, by his declaration of infinitesimal faith in the people governing and illimitable faith in The People governed. He wrote to James T. Fields,

> I hope you may have met with a little touch of Radicalism I gave them at Birmingham in the words of Buckle? With pride I observe that it makes the regular political traders, of all sorts, perfectly mad.

The direct quotation from the historian did not resolve matters, but Dickens took the opportunity to pay tribute to Buckle, "a great thinker, a great writer, and a great scholar".

Buckle related the historical development of mankind to the advancement of intellect. He did not believe in moral evolution and was not, like Comte, impressed by religious leaders; nor the political and military great men, whose influence on events was superficial and transient. His theme was how the mass of the ruled adapted to geographical and climatic conditions and gradually acquired the knowledge to civilise the natural world. He argued that "the actions of men are governed by the state of society in which they occur", and noted the statistical regularity of crimes and suicides. The assertion of causality provoked J. A.

Froude, who attacked Buckle in "The Science of History", a lecture delivered at the Royal Institution in 1864. Opposing scientific history, Froude was defending the concept of free-will. History was "a voice for ever sounding across the centuries the laws of right and wrong", and it was most often in the individual heart that the everlasting battle between good and evil was waged. The growth of industries and mechanical civilisation was of trivial consequence besides. Froude's insistence that the true history was private coincided with political pessimism:

> revolutions, reformations—those vast movements into which heroes and saints have flung themselves, in the belief that they were the dawn of the millenium—have not borne the fruit which they looked for. Milleniums are still far away.

It was a lesson of history that one did well to expect little in the way of social change.

Eliot writes in *Felix Holt* that private life is "determined by a wider public life", yet she also writes in Froude's vein as though the significance which Buckle found in statistics reduced man to an amoral puppet. Coming from an admirer of Comte, who was preoccupied with laws of development, this was surprising; but her reaction to Buckle was emotionally charged. She referred to him in 1858 as "a writer who inspires me with a personal dislike—not to put too fine a point on it, he impresses me as an irreligious, conceited man". Her hero's resolution not to profit by his father's counterfeit medicines is made in implicit defiance of the historian. Holt bypasses that "stage of speculation in which a man may doubt whether a pickpocket is blameworthy"; and takes no consolation in the view that "there must be a certain number of sneaks of robbers" in the world, so that someone else will act dishonestly even if he does not. Like Froude's, the vital interest of the novelist is finally in those matters which "are often unknown to the world" and the wider public life determining private lives is relatively static. "For the Pope Angelico is not come yet," Eliot concludes the Proem to *Romola*; and in *Felix Holt*, she writes wearily that while such eras as that of the passing of the Reform Act generate optimism, doubt and despondency follow when the expected wonders fail to materialise.

Felix Holt may be seen as an attempt to deny the validity of the scientific historian's concept of man. Holt objects to Buckle's predilection for statistics, and is himself created a free agent. Dickens invoked an unfettered free-will as a defence against democracy. *Hard Times* (1854), like *Felix Holt* a novel perplexed with fears of organised labour, attacks statistics, distorts the utilitarian ethic and is generally out of sympathy with Buckle's radicalism. The free world of the circus is detached from industrial Coketown, and the horse-riding positives are as shadowy as those realised in Eliot's hero. But if the circus is Froude's paradise of the unconditioned will, Felix Holt is its embodiment. Froude's protest against scientific history and Buckle (apparently the only scientific historian with whom he was acquainted) was quashed by John Morley in the *Fortnightly Review* in 1867:

> surely the will is no irresistible monster springing forth in full panoply, unbegotten, unconceived, having no kinship with the rest of the mind and its influences, operating without reference to anything that has gone before, or to anything that lies outside of the mysterious seat of its own spontaneous birth . . . (Froude's) belief in the power of the will has had no parallel since the days when men believed in the fable of the Echineis—a little fish which could stop the biggest of ships merely by sticking to it.

Felix Holt is precisely this montrous will: historically unbegotten, he preaches the power of will to the Sproxton miners. The historical novel's protagonist personifies the yearning to escape from history. If, as we are told, political machinery is no force for reform, neither is the new Echineis: a conclusion in which we are anticipated by George Eliot who, no longer suggesting that her hero shows a better way to change, wishes only to proclaim that change is impossible.

5

Elizabeth Gaskell: *Sylvia's Lovers* (1863)

Sylvia's Lovers deals with events in the West Riding of Yorkshire in the 1790s. Elizabeth Gaskell had won fame (and notoriety) by writing about contemporary social problems, but in her historical novel, she was still concerned with the urgent issues of her own age. E. P. Thompson remarks that "the sensibility of the Victorian middle class was nurtured in the 1790s by frightened gentry who had seen miners, potters and cutlers reading *Rights of Man . . .*", and the nurturing of the sensibility is Gaskell's theme. There was more immediate cause for English apprehension in the 1790s than the French Revolution. But even in their cautionary works, Victorian essayists and novelists tended to imply that popular revolt was an exclusively French tradition, and the 1789 Revolution, though terrible and a warning for England, could always be referred to the instability of the French temperament. In 1856, Tocqueville's *L'Ancien Régime et la Révolution* seemed to confirm the less scholarly conclusions of Walter Bagehot, who, in his *Letters on the French Coup d'État of 1851* (1852), gathered from the incidents of 1848 that of all the "circumstances so affecting political problems, by far and out of all question the most important is *national character*", and hence that French revolutions might be blamed on the essence of the national character, "a certain mobility".

By writing on the period of the French Revolution in England, where governmental oppression also provoked a response, Gaskell was exposing the myth of English stability. *Sylvia's Lovers* undermined interpretations of the past which were based on a theory of national characteristics, and the comment on the effect of the salt-tax is indicative of the novelist's approach:

> when the price of this necessary was so increased by the tax upon it as to make it an expensive, sometimes an unattainable, luxury to the working man, Government did more to demoralize the popular sense of rectitude and uprightness than heaps of sermons could undo. . . .

Gaskell continues, "it may seem curious to trace up the popular standard of truth to taxation, but I do not think the idea would be so very far-fetched". In *Felix Holt*, Eliot dissociates politics and morals, arguing that reform is useless, so long as the workers whom it is designed to benefit remain corrupt. Gaskell appreciates that morals are socially conditioned in the present, and must be influenced by political change.

There are no demagogues in *Sylvia's Lovers*. In G. P. R. James's romance, *The Jacquerie*, the French peasants are led by "a fiend incarnate, whose heart Satan must possess entirely, for he has endowed his brain with talents which are but used for the purposes of desolation and destruction". This is the standard version of the popular leader: Robespierre as he appears in Bulwer's *Zanoni*, or the Defarges in *A Tale of Two Cities*. Gaskell, too, is dealing with riot and its inspirer, but describes the rescue of the pressed sailors as "a distinctly popular movement", and Daniel Robson is spurred less by his passions than a valid sense of oppression.

Mrs Gaskell was inclined to regard the Manchester workers as children, whose impulses towards a higher humanity needed cosseting. There is Clough's story of Mrs Gaskell at the Manchester Exhibition, where she answered a policeman's query by confirming that Florence Nightingale's sister was the Crimean heroine, since "she could not bear to take away the man's faith". Clough comments that he is not anxious to read any more of Mrs Gaskell's biographies. Still, her residence in Manchester must have raised her social awareness and extended her sympathies, and it is not only in the novels of class conflict that she affirms the interdependence of politics and popular morals. There is no suggestion that dealing with the age of the press-gang, or with themes inspired by the situation in contemporary Manchester in *Mary*

Barton (1848) and *North and South* (1854–55), she is treating special cases. Writing about Cranford in the 1830s, or Hollingford in the 1820s in *Wives and Daughters* (1864–66), she does not use a closed community, as Eliot tends to do, to isolate moral issues from a wider social context. Mrs Kirkpatrick's duplicity cannot be abstracted from the presentation, in *Wives and Daughters*, of the plight of the single woman in early nineteenth-century society. "I wonder if I am to go on all my life toiling and moiling for money? It's not natural. Marriage is the natural thing; then the husband has all that kind of dirty work to do, and his wife sits in the drawing-room like a lady." In the 1790s, Sylvia Robson experiences as a disturbing innovation what by the 1820s has become the marital norm: Gaskell's sense of the progression is unerring. Indicative, surely, is the very lack of research which her historical novel entailed, compared with Eliot's labours on *Romola*, Reade's on *The Cloister and the Hearth* or, to take a novel set in the period of *Sylvia's Lovers*, even Dickens' on *A Tale of Two Cities*. "All the time I was at work on the Two Cities, I read no books but such as had the air of the time in them," he wrote to Forster. Gaskell looked up the odd Admiralty document, flicked through the *Annual Registers* of the appropriate years for references to the press-gang, and read some local history. She was not, like Eliot reading for *Felix Holt*, surprised by the material she turned up; and the past did not have to be resuscitated by toil.

In 1865, the *Saturday Review* remarked, in its obituary of Mrs Gaskell, that *Sylvia's Lovers*, while with *Cranford* considered the best of her novels, both being "still eagerly read and widely admired", was also criticised as "a very unpleasant story; and there are critics who lay down a positive canon that radically unpleasant stories had better be left unwritten". Certainly, Gaskell's audience would have been shocked by the sympathy extended to a heroine renouncing her marital vows; but anxiety for stability within the family would be tied to other fears, and one may suspect that here as in Meredith's case, the accusation of "unpleasantness" was a defence against a radical treatment of society. There are splashes of comfort for the reader, as in Gaskell's comment on the press-gang: "now all this tyranny is marvellous to us". But we are shown the process by which

Philip Hepburn's fellow-feeling is corroded by the new economic values, so that he is led to collude with the press-gang to rid himself of Kinraid, his rival for Sylvia's hand; and this novel analysing the birth of the Victorian middle-class sensibility is not calculated to isolate the past from the reader, or to make him feel virtuous in comparison with the rough old times. The *laissez-faire* attitude adopted by Hepburn to the gang's seizure of Kinraid is generalised by the 1860s: that *laissez-faire* was never unadulterated does not mean that it was an invention of Carlyle's. The whole of Manchester's miseries during the cotton famine, wrote the *Westminster Review* in 1863, "must be charged against the system which has thrown up these vast hives, without a single consideration of the commonest of human wants". The interests of the workers "have been put out of sight in the struggle of unlimited competition".

Gaskell's heroine, Sylvia, is the daughter of Daniel Robson, who farms near Monkshaven, a fishing-town on the Yorkshire coast. She is loved by her cousin, Philip Hepburn, whose industry and astuteness in Monkshaven's large drapery shop (owned by the Quaker brothers, John and Jeremiah Foster) earns him a partnership by the age of twenty-three. Unreceptive to her cousin's advances, Sylvia falls in love with the whaler, Charley Kinraid, and they are betrothed; much to the disquiet of Hepburn, who knows Kinraid's reputation as a womaniser. Philip is sent to London on the Fosters' business, and on a lonely stretch of the coast runs into Kinraid, who is joining his ship, and sees him captured by the press-gang. Overpowered, Kinraid shouts out a message for Sylvia, which Philip delays transmitting. On his return a couple of months later, he finds that Kinraid is given up for drowned, and withholds his knowledge of the truth. Later still, Daniel Robson leads an attack on the local stronghold of the press-gang to free some sailors. He is hanged in consequence, and when Sylvia and her mother are left helpless, Philip seizes the chance to press his cousin into marriage. After a year, Kinraid returns, Philip's treachery is exposed, and he leaves Sylvia and Monkshaven to enlist as a soldier. Kinraid also vanishes, and the two men meet at the siege of Acre, where Philip saves his rival's life and is hurt in an explosion aboard ship. Disfigured and penniless, he arrives in England, and lodges at the charity institution,

St Sepulchre's. Gradually, he gathers courage to return to Sylvia, whose heart has softened in the meanwhile, and who has heard of Kinraid's marriage. There is barely time for an evasive reconciliation before Philip dies.

A summary of the plot does not distinguish *Sylvia's Lovers* from the run of historical romances; but Gaskell's characters emerge as the products of their age, and Hepburn's story is not a fable illustrating the pitfalls of yielding to temptation. Gaskell is as much concerned with the particularised individual as Daniel Robson in his critique of conventional rhetoric. "Nation here! nation there! I'm a man and you're another, but nation's nowhere." The links between Robson and the nation are what the novel proceeds to investigate, and the historical gloss on Robson's stance is to be found in the works of Tom Paine, whose *Rights of Man* was published in two parts in 1791 and 1792. For Paine, the nation was not to be abstracted from all its constituents, with their antagonistic interests. In his *Letter Addressed to the Addressers* of 1792, he wrote that England was class-divided between "those who pay taxes, and those who receive and live upon taxes", and thought the celebrated Constitution an admirable one for "courtiers, placemen, pensioners, borough-holders, and the leaders of the Parties", but not "for at least ninety-nine parts of the nation out of a hundred".

In her analysis of the historical forces operating in the 1790s, Gaskell is preoccupied by the same issues as Paine, the contemporary political theorist; though with the advantage of hindsight, she does not believe free enterprise a cure for the nation's evils. The novel shows no common interest between the poor, who do the fighting, and the government prosecuting the French war. Philip Hepburn, the new man acquiring a stake in society, remarks approvingly: "John and Jeremiah Foster pay in taxes, and militiaman pays in person; and if sailors cannot pay in taxes, and will not pay in person, why they must be made to pay; and that's what th' press-gang is for. . . ." This is the logic which Burke defended in face of the French revolutionary threat, and which Paine exposed for what it was in *Rights of Man*. Burke refuses to be bashful about employing the word "mob", and indeed prides himself on the kind of English plain-speaking which is disastrously lacking in France; but Paine, and Gaskell in her novel, shun such rhetoric.

141

"It is by distortedly exalting some men, that others are distortedly debased, till the whole is out of nature," writes Paine. In *Sylvia's Lovers*, the liberation of the pressed sailors, which leads to Robson's execution at York, is for the ruling class a mob riot to be punished accordingly.

E. P. Thompson remarks of the popular pamphleteering of the 1790s that "it might almost seem that issues could be defined in five words: Burke's two-word epithet on the one hand, Paine's three-word banner on the other". The argument between advocates of the "rights of man" and those who denied rights to the "swinish multitude" extended to the 1860s. Despite his faith in free enterprise, Paine's works remained a threat to an enterprising middle class; and they were still relevant, E. J. Hobsbawm explains, because for most of Paine's readers, private enterprise offered no salvation. "His and their opposition was ostensibly against 'privilege' which stood in the way of 'freedom'; but in fact it was also against unrecognised and new forces which pushed men such as themselves into poverty." In the 1790s, according to Lord Cockburn, everything was soaked in the one event of the French Revolution: it was still a warning for Gaskell's contemporaries, and Burke retained many disciples.

To Whitwell Elwin, writing in the *Quarterly Review* in 1859, Burke's pronouncements had lost none of their force, since the ideas of John Bright were the transcript of those prevailing in 1789. Croker, the first Englishman systematically to research into the French Revolution, found that his studies progressively confirmed Burke's wisdom. In 1856, he recalled that the fall of the Bastille and the bloody scenes which followed had unfavourably impressed his parents' household: a marital alliance with Burke's family completed the Crokers' admiration for the historian, whose prophetic opinions had been "wonderfully illustrated and fulfilled" by subsequent events. The *Saturday Review* objected to Gaskell's treating in *Sylvia's Lovers* "a state of society which has passed away"; conservatives would have missed the drift of the criticism. For Gaskell, of course, times have changed. She is not concerned with parallels between the 1790s and the 1860s, but with the earlier decade as the vital prehistory of her own age. Burke's aristocratic opposition to the mob is generalised with the rise of a middle class equally nervous of popular politics.

Monkshaven in the 1790s is an open society, where an ordinary sailor might become a shipowner. The whaler, Kinraid, rises on merit; and it is true, too, that Philip Hepburn does the same in the Fosters' drapery shop, "without a penny of his own, simply by diligence, honesty, and faithful quick-sightedness. . . ." By the time that Gaskell's contemporaries were claiming that every workman might be his own capitalist, the available instances were too few to provide much encouragement. But in Monkshaven, the appearance of the press-gang, a class instrument, is felt and resented as an unwarrantable intrusion, and the anger and vengeance provoked owe nothing to madness or drink. Gaskell certainly does not accept Hepburn's apologia for the government's methods of recruitment, and sees the propagandising against the French as demagoguery of the kind that the Victorian middle class liked to attribute to popular leaders. Dispassionately, Gaskell associates law with the law-making society; and the law which backs the gang also hangs Robson at York.

The Fosters who preach against retaliation are Quakers (this is relevant beyond the Quaker predilection for pacifism) and also shopkeepers, members of the class which can "pay in taxes". As a Christian, Gaskell allows for a residue of original sin, and in the fierce men drinking in the bars, "liquor called forth all the desperate, bad passions of human nature". But the congregations in the bars are incited by the press-gang's activity, and the wild and desperate portion of the Monkshaven population cannot be dismissed as roughs who will join any fray for the excitement: their rebellion is widely supported. Paine admonished his opponent Burke for implying that the French Revolution "burst forth like a creation from a chaos", and Buckle was still needing to remind Gaskell's contemporaries that the patience by which the Revolution was so long deferred was more astonishing than its final outbreak. Whereas Dickens and Eliot, in their historical novels, overreact to individual excesses, Gaskell's is a radical analysis, and she remarks that in Monkshaven too, the more aware spirits were only surprised that the explosion did not happen sooner than it did. Certainly, she described the destruction of the Randyvowse as "mad work", but her readers had also to recognise that the acquiescent Philip Hepburn reports the justices as "mad for vengeance". The working class has not a monopoly of passion, and

143

that of the justices is calculated, aroused at the least threat to the "nation" existing only for courtiers and placemen. Robson spares time in the midst of the attack to give money to the wretched Simpson, who has served the press-gang: his revenge is more humane than the rule to which he is subjected.

Still, the shift in values has historical causes, and Monkshaven is part of England, not a Shangri-La. The "love-interest" in *Sylvia's Lovers*, so far from being the core of the romance with history as lush backcloth in the G. P. R. James fashion, illumines and is dependent upon the conditions of a particularised society. Charley Kinraid the whaler, the lover favoured by Sylvia's father, belongs to the old dispensation. The prudential shopkeeping Hepburn, favoured by the mother who has demeaned herself socially in marrying Robson, represents the new. Socially as well as romantically, Sylvia is delicately poised between the two: she is a landgirl who, influenced by her mother, is too much the young lady for the neighbours' taste. The personal-historical choice facing Sylvia is emblemised when she has to pick material for a new cloak. Her father wants her to buy a flamboyant red; her mother and Hepburn, the more practical grey, "a respectable, quiet-looking article". Sylvia rejects the grey as initially she rejects the respectable Hepburn, but her power to choose is limited. To mollify her mother, Sylvia compromises by buying less material than she really needs, and she is later to compromise more drastically in marrying Hepburn.

Her fluctuating social allegiance puts Sylvia in the tradition of the Waverley heroes. In an essay of 1856, Bagehot complained of the great Scottish novels that their central figure was "frequently not their most interesting topic". But Scott well understood their committed hero's tendency to obscure those forces whose mediation through individual lives the historical novelist portrayed. Gaskell's Sylvia, like Waverley (and like Paul Manning in *Cousin Phyllis*, written in 1863) drifts between the old order and the new, and bears the marks of each. To his credit, Hepburn is a valuable friend because of his managerial efficiency, which is in demand after the arrest of Sylvia's father. Both Robson and Kinraid can act fecklessly and irresponsibly.

Kinraid tells Sylvia that he has always spent his money freely; Hepburn, in his cousin's eyes, is "full o' business and the shop, and o' making money, and getting wealth". Sylvia is unjust, but trade seems to her a prosaic occupation compared with the natural rhythms of work at the farm, and Gaskell indicates that the Fosters' shop is a recent development at Monkshaven. The house-wives and Sylvia herself barter their goods in open market, and are dispirited if there is a remnant to be sold off to the shops. Still, there is no deep division between the customs of Monkshaven, like face-to-face bargaining, and the entrepreneurial activities of the shopkeepers; and the Fosters' drapery shop is a centre of com-munal life. E. P. Thompson writes that the legal code and the unwritten popular code have seldom been so distinct from one another as they were in the later eighteenth century. The Fosters still relate closely to the popular code, which accepted their deal-ing in smuggled goods. Although they run a bank in conjunction with the shop, they do not charge their customers interest, mak-ing their money by speculating on the capital (itself, though, a novel venture). The brothers are reluctant to abandon business transactions based on trust, and ashamed of sending Hepburn to investigate the defaulting London merchant.

It is suggested, however, that commercial accommodation with popular life will be transitory. Hepburn's journey to London marks the beginning of a new era and, appropriately, initiates his treach-ery to Kinraid. The Fosters are shocked by the merchant's perfidy, since he is "publicly distinguished for his excellent and philan-thropic character". Already, middle-class philanthropy appears under a shadow, one that lengthens through the nineteenth cen-tury: in *Little Dorrit*, Pancks denounces the patriarchal Casby as "a philanthropic sneak". The Fosters themselves, while disin-terestedly handing over the shop to their assistants, are leaving to carry on the bank as a self-sufficient institution, rather than as an adjunct to the drapery business and run more or less as a service to their customers. Here are the beginnings of that capitalist specialisation and concentration which in turn so disastrously narrowed the lives of the workers. "At the time of which I write, there was but little division of labour in the Monkshaven whale fishery," notes Gaskell. By 1853, Ruskin was writing in "The Nature of Gothic" that his generation had "much studied and much per-fected, of late, the great civilized invention of the division of labour; only we give it a false name. It is not, truly speaking, the labour that is divided; but the men. . . ." The Fosters show an inclination to subdue the independence of their assistants to their own commercial interest. They think it "a good thing for the shop" that Hepburn and Coulson should equip themselves with wives; and disapprove of Hepburn's marrying Sylvia since she is barely respectable as the daughter of a hanged man, and might injure trade.

It is significant that the shopkeeping Fosters should be Quakers. E. P. Thompson remarks of the Quakers that by the 1790s, "they had prospered too much: . . . the continuing tradition, at its best, gave more to the social conscience of the middle class than to the popular movement". In her portrayal of the Fosters and also of Philip Hepburn, not a Quaker himself but sharing, we are told, the sect's "austere distrust of a self-seeking spirit", Gaskell is showing how the Puritan virtues were successfully applied to commerce. The *Saturday Review* commented on the development in 1858.

> Industry and honesty, being recognised and practised as duties, lead to wealth; and by degrees the inner light to which at first these virtues were merely humble though indispensable adjuncts, becomes more and more exceptional and transitory. The morality remains, and brings in its train riches, and often harshness and worldliness far harder than those of ordinary men of the world, because those who indulge them always reflect that if it would but shine (as it possibly may), there is always the inner light to fall back upon.

There appeared in 1865, also in the *Saturday Review*, a leader on "Quakerism and Bright", which was critical of the Quakers:

> . . . they are thought of with a sort of contemptuous toleration as an evanescent sect, which has exchanged its first fervour for a very consistent devotion to the arts of commerce. . . . The cultivation of the commercial spirit by the Quakers is the most awkward feature in their history as a religious body; and we can scarcely understand how Fox and the eloquent Barclay would recognise the depositaries of the Indwelling Light in the great discount houses, and flourishing banks, and breweries of our time. . . .

Bright's politics were offensive enough, but at least true to the tradition of George Fox, whence the radical leader "learned his hatred of Church and State as they now are, and—most pitiful, but in Quakerism intelligible and even consistent—his pitting class against class. . . ." Bright was indeed conscious of his Quaker milieu, which influenced as well his adherence to the principles of *laissez-faire* economics, since interference from the state (or from trade-unions) in the relations between capitalist and workman was repugnant to his Quaker notions of equality and freedom. In her sympathetic study of the Fosters, Gaskell foreshadows the broad development of nineteenth-century Quakerism. Astutely, she describes Jeremiah Foster elucidating the accounts of the shop to Hepburn and Coulson, the other assistant, preliminary to their succession. It was Jeremiah's daily custom to read a chapter of the Bible to his housekeeper: "and, like many, he reserved a peculiar tone for that solemn occupation,—a tone which he unconsciously employed for the present enumeration of pounds, shillings, and pence".

Philip Hepburn, Sylvia's lover and the Fosters' shopman, two generations younger than the Fosters, is more dissociated from the popular life around him. Economically and emotionally, he is more sophisticated, and it is indicative that he is not a Quaker, though raised by Friends. The sect blended paternalism with the practice of *laissez-faire*, and in *Past and Present*, Carlyle commends "Friend Prudence the good Quaker", whose virtue, however, is rewarded on earth.

> Prudence keeps a thousand workmen; has striven in all ways to attach them to him; has provided conversational soirées; playgrounds, bands of music for the young ones; went even "the length of buying them a drum"; all of which has turned out to be an excellent investment.

Married to Sylvia, Hepburn throws off Quaker influences. A churchwardenship is a certificate of respectability, and to gain one, he attends church twice on Sundays: Gaskell questions how far he would have been as regular in his worship where he was not known. Daniel Robson, we hear, never worried about his popularity, "still less whether he was respected", and in their loss of spontaneity, all Hepburn's relations are opposed to those obtaining at the farm, where the labourer Kester is treated nearly, though not quite, like one of the family. Hepburn scolds Sylvia for shaking hands with a girl he supposes to be common, or worse, in the exultation following the return of the whalers, and is ever anxious to shield his cousin from the contamination of the town, although she is at her ease there.

Hepburn is separated both from the Fosters, with their diversified interests, and the housewives, haggling over their wares in the market. He swings himself over the counter "after the fashion of shopmen". In *Religion and the Rise of Capitalism*, R. H. Tawney shows how those who disparaged the significance of the social fabric tended towards a callous regard for the poor. Convinced that character is all and circumstances nothing, the Puritan

> sees in the poverty of those who fall by the way, not a misfortune to be pitied and relieved, but a moral failing to be condemned, and in riches, not an object of suspicion—though like other gifts they may be abused—but the blessing which rewards the triumph of energy and will.

Here is an explanation of Hepburn's sensitive class-consciousness, and also of his disastrous marriage. Although he is interested in winning riches primarily as a condition of winning his cousin, his monetary attitudes colour the relationship, and Sylvia takes on the aspect of something that can be bought, or at least earned, the blessing rewarding "the triumph of energy and will". She will be won, as Hepburn won the shop, through "patient self-restraint", and his references to his cousin are run through with economic metaphor: Sylvia must not be "cheapened", she must be married "at any cost". As religious energy is diverted to commerce and used to gain wealth, so it permeates the pursuit of Sylvia, who is to be "shrined in the dearest sanctuary of his being"; a discarded title for the novel was "Philip's Idol". Hepburn's worship of Sylvia is an undercutting of her humanity, and by putting a price-tag on the beloved, he is adopting the values of the press-gang: "men must be had at any price of money, or suffering, or of injustice". Sylvia becomes the proto-Victorian wife, the sexless doll, whose susceptible purity must be defended from the world. She is a plaything: "one pretty soft little dove was somehow perpetually associated in his mind with the idea of his cousin Sylvia". Traditionally, the dove is a symbol of peace, and the wife comes to promise peace from commercial cares. Married to Hepburn, Sylvia must be a lady, whose distinction is that she does no work for her living: work is a drudgery to be escaped, and the wife's leisure a mark of her husband's economic prestige. Stifled, Sylvia resorts to long walks by the cliffs.

The deprecatory attitude to work is incongruous in Monkshaven, where work is the main source of identity. This is true at the Haytersbank farm and aboard Kinraid's whaler, but neither pursuit allows for defined periods of leisure, and each incorporates the sense of wonder which Sylvia misses in her marriage. When Hepburn watches the press-gang capture Kinraid, his heart is steeled by the sound of his rival whistling "Weel may the keel row", so soon after parting with Sylvia. For Kinraid, however, there is no severance between his feelings for Sylvia and his work, and another possible title for the novel was "The Specksioneer". The song itself is a lullaby accepting work and its hazards as integral to life, and is chanted by the girls of Monkshaven as they welcome home the whalers; but Hepburn considers such girls common, and the whistling strikes him as callous.

Gaskell claims that men and women in the 1790s possessed an emotional unity lacking in her own age. Sylvia was content to admire Hester Rose's goodness in sitting with the bed-ridden sister of Darley, the sailor shot by the press-gang, without herself feeling guilty. But in 1863, there are many

> fully conscious of their virtues, qualities, failings, and weaknesses, and who go about comparing others with themselves—not in a spirit of Pharisaism and arrogance, but with a vivid self-consciousness that more than anything else deprives characters of freshness and originality.

In the course of the novel, Sylvia acquires the attributes of the modern young lady, "an eminently artificial thing—the result of forced repression in some directions, unnatural stimulation in others", as John Stuart Mill described her in *The Subjection of Women*, written in 1861. Invited to dine with her husband at the Fosters', Sylvia is bemused by the requisite gentilities, and for the first time endures the self-consciousness that tormented some of Gaskell's contemporaries. Mill was a main sufferer, as he relates in Chapter V of the *Autobiography*, until he was soothed by the poetry of Wordsworth, and evolved an outlook akin to Carlyle's "antiself-consciousness theory". Carlyle wrote wistfully in *Past and Present* of the Middle Ages, when religion was not yet "a diseased self-introspection, an agonising inquiry", and Ruskin told his generation in 1870 that "*we* cannot design, because we have too much to think of, and we think of it too anxiously".

Thomas Hughes's Tom Brown becomes introspective at Oxford, and in some measure it is a consequence of his Rugby education. Like the Puritans, Dr Arnold had preached the individual's direct accountability to God, and a closed community like Rugby was able to channel Tom's moral zeal. There, he was "rather a great man", and it is the "responsibility" which he misses at Oxford. The complexities of nineteenth-century society meant that the would-be crusader was hard put to find an unequivocal cause. Himself saved from self-doubt by a reading of *Past and Present*, Tom writes to an old Rugbeian friend at Cambridge who, like Milton's devils, has fallen to the pondering of necessity and free-will, sternly to condemn the habitual "groping about amongst one's own sensations, and ideas, and whimsies of one kind and an-another". Matthew Arnold and Clough were real products of Thomas Arnold's Rugby, and Matthew's criticism of Clough was like Brown's of his Cambridge friend:

> you would never take your assiette as something determined final and unchangeable for you and proceed to work away on the basis of that: but were always poking and patching and cobbling at the assiette itself. . . .

It was from Clough foremost amongst his friends that Arnold felt urged to protect himself by the insouciant mask of dandyism. He believed it the doom of his poetic faculty to expose himself to the conflicting currents of nineteenth-century thought, and was afraid of those whom he suspected of trying to make him a "reformer". If the poet succumbed to the adoption of an intellectual stance, certain to set him at odds with most of his fellows, he would (as Lionel Trilling paraphrases Arnold's argument) "lose the deep, sure insight which is the prime power of the poet, which comes from integration, proportion and joy but, above all, from a certain unconsciousness. . . ." Of course, Arnold was unable to protect his poetry from Victorian disunity, and Empedocles was reduced to "a devouring flame of thought". When in his opening lecture as Professor of Poetry at Oxford,

Arnold spoke of "depression and *ennui*" as characteristics of modern literature, he included his own poetry in the indictment.

Sylvia Robson has been fascinated by ladylike vanities, until they are "burnt out of her by the hot iron of acute suffering", a taste of the misery which changing attitudes to trade are inflicting on the mass of the community. His treachery once revealed, Sylvia cannot feel for her husband until he, too, has been purged by suffering. In his *Lectures on Art* of 1870, Ruskin remarked of the Middle Ages that "the very eventfulness of the life rendered it careless, as generally is still the case with soldiers and sailors". Hepburn becomes a soldier, like Kinraid's an occupation conferring identity, and also neatly expressive of the Puritan view of the elect at war with the world. Deprived of an economic outlet for his aggression, Hepburn turns it against the French. Unfortunately, the novel's historical perspective blurs in the presentation of the war, and although Hepburn's gallant soldiering is meant as a social integration of his drives, the English are made to seem a racial elect: Gaskell is as elitist as the Puritans. There was indeed an upsurge of anti-Gallican sentiment in the mid-1790s, and she is careful to indicate that for Kinraid, what his officers tell him is good enough. Still, the war is conveyed as a series of random heroics on the part of the English; and to accommodate an incongruous moral, the Christian notion of possible redemption for the greatest of sinners. A latitudinarian providence watches over Hepburn, who is allowed to save his rival's life at the siege of Acre.

After the rescue, Hepburn is blown up in an accident. On his return to England, scarred and hopeless, he finds temporary lodging at St Sepulchre's, where he is a victim of his own former prejudices: the charity of the charity institution stops short of treating its inmates as individuals. This is, perhaps, too appropriate, and what is wrong is the didactic intention, that those who live by class attitudes shall also suffer by them. Doubtless they will, but not by a simple reversal of roles. Hepburn's career becomes a pilgrim's progress, where moral lessons are engraved on the heart.

Back in Monkshaven, Hepburn is tended in his distress by the sister of his old enemy, Kester. While Sylvia regards the anonymous stranger as a vagrant, she advocates turning him adrift, giving "cautious and prudent" advice to the widow, the values absorbed from her mother and reinforced by her marriage. This is a time of famine, and though the rich deny themselves, their contributions are "drops in the ocean of the great want of the people"; the situation is similar to Manchester's during the cotton famine in process while Gaskell wrote. That Hepburn has no money is for the widow a good reason for not repulsing him. "To a more calculating head", it might have suggested the opposite, and Sylvia is converted from such calculation by an old woman whose values are not economically based. Once the vagrant is seen as human, Sylvia's pity is aroused, and she can still sympathise when he is revealed as her husband. She gains the clue to his identity through discovering his pawned watch with the watchmaker, an exemplary character. With capital for expansion, comments Gaskell, "he might have been a rich man; but it is to be doubted whether he would have been as happy. . . ." Where wealth and guilt are inseparable—"the persons who become rich are, generally speaking, industrious, resolute, proud, covetous, prompt, methodical, sensible, unimaginative, insensitive, and ignorant", wrote Ruskin in *Unto this Last* (1860–62)—it is safer to live modestly. Compassion is adulterated in the 1790s. Sylvia, passing Hepburn in the street while ignorant of his identity, persuades her daughter to offer the poor man a cake; but the child is bribed by the promise of another one, "twice as big". Philanthropy was later to become a class weapon of those who made sure of the poor's continued dependence on charity.

Here is a complexity at odds with the pilgrim's progress of Hepburn, and it is not expected that moral lessons will nullify the heart's history. Subtly presented, too, is the scene of Sylvia's reconciliation with Hepburn, whose sacrifice in saving the child of their marriage from drowning helps to placate his wife. Sylvia has heard of Kinraid's hasty marriage after his last departure, and comforts her husband with the assurance that the whaler was "faithless and fickle", just as Hepburn had maintained. Actually the marriage is the reverse of a confirmation of his clear judgment. Kinraid has married disillusioned with Sylvia's calculating union, and wilfully adopting her criteria. He aims for social and financial advantage, and his wife is the doll that Hepburn tried to make of Sylvia, a "pretty, joyous, prosperous little bird of a woman". Sylvia needs to deceive herself as well as Hepburn: her enlightenment is partial.

The later chapters are disappointing, however, since Gaskell is evasive as well as her characters. Sylvia, never before impressed by dogma, begins to worry about her heavenly prospects, and nursing her husband, is described as "upborne from earth". At the close, material developments are divested of relationship with the human heart:

> Monkshaven is altered now into a rising bathing-place. Yet, standing near the site of widow Dobson's house on a summer's night . . . you may hear the waves come lapping up the shelving shore with the same ceaseless, ever-recurrent sound as that which Philip listened to in the pauses between life and death.

The movement forward in time to a changed Monkshaven, and the novelist's taking notes for the story, seems promising: it is included to establish a timeless perspective on history. There is no placing of Hester Rose's charity in founding alms-houses for disabled sailors and soldiers, though St Sepulchre's, and the charity of the rich which is like a drop in the ocean, have been criticised. That Quakers had prospered, and at best contributed to the social conscience of the middle class, is not Gaskell's point, and Christian gestures pass at face value.

Hepburn has justified his silence about Kinraid's forced enlistment through a providential interpretation of history, and Gaskell too becomes a fatalist, but there is still the suggestion of an historical base for her gloom. The class-conscious Hepburn is disfigured in the explosion, and mortally injured in rescuing his daughter. Finally acceptable again to Sylvia, he has lost his life as well as his looks; a savage humanisation, but comparable to Gaskell's treatment of the mill-owner Carson in *Mary Barton*, where she seems to sense the inadequacy of her personalised solution even while she propounds it. His son's assassination shows the ruthless capitalist to be human after all, flesh and blood of his workers. But Carson emerges less as the capitalist humanised than the capitalist destroyed, "no longer the enemy, the oppressor, but a very poor, and desolate old man".

The main characters in *Mary Barton* leave for Canada; and in a long Quaker tradition, and having inherited the Fosters' fortune to ease local difficulties, the child saved by Hepburn goes to America, the great new democracy. In *Beauchamp's Career* (1875) , Meredith's hero drowns in the Solent rescuing the working-class child, "the insignificant bit of mudbank life", but fitter to survive than the gentlemanly radical. Doubting whether capitalists can be humanised, Gaskell cannot envisage alternatives to the *laissez-faire* ethic whose propagation has been her theme, and takes refuge in religiosity, or in emigration, which is a mark of her despair. But there is an interesting sentence describing Hepburn's consciousness in the last moments. "All the temptations that had beset him rose clearly before him; the scenes themselves stood up in their solid materialism—he could have touched the places; the people, the thoughts, the arguments that Satan had urged in behalf of sin, were reproduced with the vividness of a present time." Here it is not only Hepburn who is invoking Satan; but for Gaskell, Satan is still more than half-rooted in history.

6

George Meredith: *Sandra Belloni* (1864) and *Vittoria* (1866)

The Italian adventures of Meredith's heroine, who is born
Emilia Alessandra Belloni, must be read in the context of her
earlier experience, the subject of *Sandra Belloni*, or "Emilia in
England". Here, though, I am especially concerned with *Vittoria*,
or "Emilia in Italy", a portrayal of Italy in 1848. *Vittoria* was
Meredith's prophecy against empire, British as well as Austrian.
Despite its own empire, the English ruling class tended to roman-
ticise the enemies of imperialism. The assumption was that the
oppressed nationalities were fighting for the liberties which England already possessed, and there was a paternal interest in
England's emulators. When it too evidently appeared that England was not the model, and that freedom from foreign despotism
was a prelude to social reconstruction, sympathy was qualified;
though, according to English opinion, the extremists were a few
malignant men, who beguiled their followers to ruin. The villain
of the Italian Risorgimento, Meredith's theme in *Sandra Belloni*
and *Vittoria*, was Mazzini, who was denounced as a red republican and urged, when his country was unified under a constitutional monarchy, to sacrifice party shibboleths to patriotism.
While Garibaldi was lionised on his English visit in 1864, *The
Times*, wary of his tumultous reception by the workers, had
stressed that "we have no grievances of our own for Garibaldi to
redress"; and he was pitied for isolated fanaticism when he
challenged Piedmont. Whether the freedom sought by the Italians
had prevailed in England, or constitutional monarchy would be
an Italian panacea, were open questions to the radical Meredith.

Meredith wrote to his friend Captain Maxse in 1878 that the English "present hugging of India, which they are ruling for the sake of giving a lucrative post to the younger sons of their middle class, is a picture for mankind". Wilfrid Pole, when he is introduced in *Sandra Belloni*, has just returned from soldiering in India, and it is appropriate that he should later serve with the Austrians in Italy. Meredith's alertness to the kinship between imperial England and imperial Austria made *Sandra Belloni* and *Vittoria* vastly superior to the many other contemporary novels about the Risorgimento. These abound in the confusions which alone allowed the monied classes in England to assume a democratic pose. In *Half a Million of Money* (1865), Amelia Blandford Edwards is equally fervent for Italian nationalism and the British Empire. Looking back over the preceding century, she remarks, "we lost America, it is true; but we conquered India, we annexed the Canadas, and we colonized New Zealand and Australia". Margaret Roberts, in *Mademoiselle Mori* (1860), ingenuously compares the Italian response to oppression with the hysteria which seized the English during the Indian Mutiny.

Individually, Meredith found the Austrian officers "gentlemanly men". Meredith's claim to have done justice to both sides in the war reflected more than a model impartiality. He had a weakness for gentlemen, and in *Sandra Belloni* and *Vittoria*, the shadowy figure of Merthyr Powys is testimony that the gentlemanly values sometimes escaped critical analysis. English attitudes to the Risorgimento were generally ambivalent, and though both novelists were sympathetic not merely to Italian unification but to republicanism, we may suspect that the Austrians had the appeal for Meredith that they did for Dickens. Writing from Italy in 1853, Dickens allowed that the Austrians would always respond to being treated "like gentlemen", and remarked, "now, the Austrian police are very strict, but they really know how to do business, and they do it". Obviously, opposition in England to those who were gentlemanly and businesslike would have been accorded scant sympathy, and there is a hint here that Italian enthusiasm was the vicarious rebellion of men who were in small danger of becoming firebrands at home. Victorian radicalism, like Victorian philanthropy, often went abroad. But Meredith's vaunted impartiality is not very damaging in *Vittoria*, where he makes the connections which otherwise he was inclined to overlook. "The deteriorating state of a perpetual repressive force", as Meredith describes the Austrian presence in *Sandra Belloni*, is shown to make brutes even of gentlemen. The imperial dilemma is that of the Austrian officer, Weisspreiss, persuaded by his aristocratic fiancée to duel with a series of Italian challengers as an assertion of national supremacy. Weary of his role, Weisspreiss "wanted peace; but as he also wanted Countess Anna of Lenkenstein and her estates, it may possibly be remarked of him that what he wanted he did not want to pay for".

Meredith's analysis of individuals owes nothing to theories of national characteristics, and members of both the English and Italian ruling classes emerge as closer in sensibility to the Austrians than to the Italian revolutionaries. Meredith wrote as late as 1907 that

> society is kept in animation by the customary, in the first place, and secondly by sentiment. It has little love of Earth (or Nature) and gives ear mainly to those who shiver with dread of the things that are, not seeing that a frank acceptance of Reality is the firm basis of the Ideal.

Preparing to change society, the Chief (Meredith's portrait of Mazzini) bases his Ideal on the Real, and on Motterone, "finds his clustered visions . . . confronting the strange, beloved visible life". The English intruders, Vittoria's old associates, view nature aesthetically, as they do art. They are self-conscious tourists to whom nature is a pleasant diversion and human presence (Italian presence in Italy) a blot on the scenery. In both *Vittoria* and *Sandra Belloni*, Meredith reverses his countrymen's critique of foreign radicals. Mazzini and other exiles were censured by the English press as dreamers, sustained by a small circle of sycophants: like so many spiders, the agitators wove their webs of fanatical doctrine. "Their heart," commented *The Times* sternly in 1856, "has ceased to beat in harmony with the pulse of the nation which they affect to represent." Meredith sees the monied classes in England precisely as *The Times* sees its exiles, so that the Italians in their single-minded devotion to the national cause become the practical men, and the English hopelessly impractical. Not the exiles, but those who rule without representing England, are forced into fantasy. Meredith expands in the Italian novels A. O. Rutson's observation in *Essays on Reform*: "with a privileged order, every question that may possibly affect their privilege is a 'dangerous' question. The privilege itself takes a place in their minds to which everything else is subordinated".

The career of Wilfrid Pole, a representative member of the middle class, is shown in bizarre detail in *Vittoria*. His sisters have changed through marriage a name smirched with the disgrace of bankruptcy, one of "the things that are" in society. Wilfred has taken the surname of his uncle, General Pierson, who is serving with the Austrians and has secured his nephew's commission. The instability of the middle-class identity is emblemised; though Adela Pole, now Mrs Sedley and wife of a gouty "millionaire city-of-London merchant", the image of her father before his downfall, condemns Vittoria's patriotic change from the old Sandra Belloni as "fantastic". During the war, Wilfrid and the Italian aristocrat, Rinaldo Guidascarpi, are imprisoned by the plebeian revolutionary, Barto Rizzo, and enabled to escape through the passion of Barto's wife for Rinaldo. Though she risks Barto's stern vengeance, Wilfrid is moved only by his personal discomfort: "the vileness of wearing one shirt two months and more had hardened his heart". Wilfrid can pretend to nonchalance during the Milanese uprising through his carelessness of the issue: the fighting seems a charade. "He had no arms, nothing but a huge white umbrella, under which he walked dry in the heavy rain, and passed through the fire like an impassive spectator of queer events." Wilfrid's eccentric pose is typically English, Meredith reminds us, and also a faithful reflection of how the English middle class views the making of history, that sequence of "queer events". "I see no hope but in a big convulsion to bring a worthy people forth," wrote Meredith to Captain Maxse in 1868. "The monied class sees the same, and reads it—will do anything to avoid it—will eat Historicus's words and him rather than accept the challenge he provokes."

Jack Lindsay has remarked on the subtlety of Meredith's portrayal of the conflicting interests within the Risorgimento. Carlo Ammiani cannot argue with his mother, the Countess, when she urges "that the nobles should be elected to lead, if they consented to lead; for if they did not lead, were they not excluded from the movement?" The repetition conveys the aristocratic clinging to the past and Carlo renounces his title, but not the obsession. Though partly admirable, his sense of responsibility for those committed to the ill-conceived Brescian expedition derives from "a profound conviction of his quality as leader". The aristocrats are prone to an indulgent fatalism. Rinaldo Guidascarpi, whose dedication deters his fellow-prisoner Wilfrid from feeling a "peculiar distinction from the common herd", is very conscious of his own. "He spoke of stars and a destiny. He cited minor events of his life to show the ground of his present belief in there being a written destiny for each individual man." Nervously, the Italian aristocrats assert their identity in the face of the mass-movement; and it is Meredith's criticism of Wilfrid and Rinaldo that, though on opposite sides in the war, they should be united against the popular leader, Barto Rizzo, and that their shared gentlemanly values should be more perceptible than their official differences. A mark of Carlo Ammiani's clear vision at the end is his abjuring of "stupid fatalism", and his appreciation that "the Fates are within us".

Like the Austrians and the English press, the Italian aristocracy distorts the Republican movement which seems to threaten privilege. Count Serabiglione, a collaborator with the Austrians, thinks Mazzini an Old Man of the Mountain, source of Italian sorrows and lusting after the smell of blood. English novelists, too, could not comprehend the nature of the popular revolution. Margaret Roberts' idea of the masses in *Mademoiselle Mori* was the same as George Eliot's in *Felix Holt*. Possessed of a tigerish nature, they want strong excitement. They exist only to be manipulated, and the hope of Rome lies in the timely advent of the "great man". The authoress, and those of her characters who favour moderation, are staunch supporters of Piedmont, and the failure of the monarchical initiative is simply explained: "distrust in their leaders, and in the noble Charles Albert, was studiously sown in the Piedmontese army by Austrian agents, or by miserable men who preferred seeing Italy enslaved to seeing her owe her independence to a king". Charles Albert, the providential great man, is to be the maker of Italy; if the unmanageable populace will consent to be managed. Meredith is more critical of the monarch, devoid of the passion alarming the aristocracy at the opera to signal the Milanese rising: it is something which, impressed mainly by what he has to lose, he is not in a position to understand. He will head an united Italy only to ensure against radical change.

Vittoria, though a plebeian by birth, must be politically educated in the course of the struggle like the aristocrats. She achieves maturity not at the end of *Sandra Belloni* (despite her self-assurance: "I see the faults. Nothing vexes me"), but at the end of *Vittoria*, though the reader may be less impressed than Meredith by that final maturity. At the beginning of the novel, Vittoria is confident that her spontaneous sense of the virtuous will coincide with patriotic service, and thinks that she can shame spies out of their calling with appeals to their better nature. Her rashness makes her a liability, and in her effort to protect her English friends, whose class bond with the Austrian enemy is ignored, she unwittingly betrays the Milanese conspiracy. In England, Vittoria has saved the Poles from ruin by raising money from the millionaire and aesthete, Pericles, binding herself in return to study for three years at the Conservatorio in Milan. Amid revolution, she pursues an art financed by the monied classes, the foes of Italy's freedom. Vittoria finds out the impossibility of doubling the roles of prima donna and revolutionary. Her art is nullified as much as her war effort, persistently sabotaged by her patron Pericles, who tries to prevent Vittoria starring in the politically-charged first night at La Scala, and kidnaps her on the way to nurse with the Piedmontese army. Pericles associates easily with the Austrians, and ironically, it is through his political obliviousness that the production of "Camilla" is able to proceed, since he is entrusted with the responsibilities of censorship. The aesthete denies art's connection with anything so vulgar, in both senses, as the national cause.

The test of Vittoria's revolutionary commitment comes when to save an aristocratic partisan, Angelo Guidascarpi, from the Austrians, she must be helped by Wilfrid Pierson, once romantically involved with her in England and now renewing his spasmodic attentions. Vittoria is still innocent enough to believe that glorious ends may be attained through the exclusive use of glorious means, and when Wilfrid attempts some characteristic emotional blackmail, the necessity for pragmatism disgusts her. It is George

Eliot's thesis that political activity breeds the degradation of private principle; and Carlyle and Dickens see the guillotining of French aristocrats not as a defensive measure which circumstances urged on a besieged republic, but as symbolising the moral bankruptcy of the Revolution. Vittoria, in her too tender regard for Wilfrid, also takes the limited view, and her temporary reluctance to demean herself overrules the wish to save Angelo and Italy. Meredith has raised the Chief for his broad perspective: "such a man, perceiving a devout end to be reached, might prove less scrupulous in his course, possibly, and less remorseful, than revolutionary generals". He is not in awe of the abstractions tainted with hypocrisy amidst the discords of class society. Most English novelists were fond of opposing their characters' patriotic duty to an instinctive sense of right, but in Swinburne's *Lesbia Brandon*, Count Mariani, an exiled disciple of Mazzini, tells an English admirer that one should be ready to give one's honour for the cause.

Themes of *Sandra Belloni* and *Vittoria* are suggested by an essay of 1865 in the *Westminster Review*, "Personal Representation", commenting on the ruling class in Parliament. "Foreigners, or the working classes, are to them, like women, not exactly fellow-creatures, but a kind of animal whom they have never dreamt of considering as on a level with themselves, nor, therefore, as altogether human." Meredith did not expect to change women's subjugated condition by educating the slavemasters, whose attitudes were socially determined. "What sort of progress is this," asked E. S. Beesly in 1869, "in which the larger part of the community remains as miserable, if not more miserable, than in a state of barbarism?" The question was often posed, evoking guilt and fear, and an urge to detach the life of the home from a problematic workaday world. In his domestic relations, at least, the male could display the benevolence which was an economic vice, and his preferred helpmate was sometimes the natural fool, who escaped the slow stain of commerce and preserved the home as an immaculate retreat. Like Coventry Patmore's "Angel in the House", the wife was idealised beyond common concerns.

In *Sandra Belloni*, Meredith portrays the Pole sisters as willing collaborators in the etherealising of their sex, though the assumption that their rank derives from providence is undermined, and its true foundation seen to be their father's precarious fortune. Meredith is reaffirming women's relationship with the world. A subversive influence at Brookfield is Sandra Belloni, the future Vittoria, of plebeian origins and mixed Welsh and Italian ancestry: she is adopted as an artistic pet, but cannot observe the Fine Shades with which the sisters evade reality. In *Vittoria*, Agostino remarks that his operatic heroine has been given "all the brains, which is a modern idea, quite!" Meredith is as generous with his own heroine, who lends plausibility to the Chief's claim that women may contribute invaluably to the success of the republican cause. When she is entrusted with signalling the Milanese rising, Carlo Ammiani protests in the terms that come easily to an aristocrat, or to members of the English middle class: "what can defenceless creatures do?" Married to Vittoria, he plays the heavy-handed Italian husband, and the aristocratic need to dominate, making Carlo no more than an imagined democrat, separates him from his admired wife and ensures his doom. Piqued by Vittoria's independence, he falls to the traitress, Violetta, who persuades him to the Brescian venture. Vittoria blames herself for not communicating her distrust of Violetta, but reasonably fears that Carlo, with his slighting view of her sex, would suspect jealousy.

Meredith's is a lucid analysis of aspects of the Risorgimento, and the English response to the Risorgimento. Despite a reputation for cynicism, he does not generally subscribe to George Eliot's linking maturity with personal and social compromise. George Eliot, however, might have approved the conclusion to *Vittoria*, and Meredith is less than consistent in the presentation of his characters. Perhaps curiously, the ambivalent attitudes of the novelist to the Risorgimento are akin to those socially and historically located in the novel. Rather like his heroine, Meredith sometimes falls into merely conventional assumptions: one way of confirming the novel's demonstration of the power of class-conditioning.

Vittoria is more ambitious, but less coherent, than *Sandra Belloni*, which does not deal with militancy between classes and expose Meredith's very mixed feelings about democracy. Here he is able to evade contemplation of the tendencies of his social criticism. Meredith declines to individualise the Pole sisters, whose lack of character aptly reflects the conditioning to which they have been subjected. But the sisters are more sharply defined than Meredith's rustics, with their excess of natural vitality. A foil for the fanciful humours imputed to, or projected on to, the mob, but composing the emotional life of the middle class, the green innocence of the lower orders freed Meredith to dissect the middle-class sensibility with his usual gusto. In *Vittoria*, however, where the lower orders fighting the war are not susceptible to stylisation, his unresolved attitudes to democracy are more troublesome. The ruling class is confronted not with pastoral but revolution, and Meredith's social analysis is correspondingly enfeebled. His own lurking fear of Barto Rizzo is very like what he has shown to be the aristocratic Carlo Ammiani's response to the plebeian revolutionary. Partly admiring Barto, Meredith cannot do him consistent justice, and does more than justice to his class enemies.

Barto Rizzo is right that Vittoria acts treacherously in alerting her English friends, and whether or not she is a conscious traitress is a less urgent issue. Barto's general reliability is emphasised. He is responsible for the despised warning to Giacomo Piaveni which would have saved the patriot's life, and that Barto is Vittoria's accuser momentarily turns her friend Laura, Giacomo's widow, against her. A plebeian, Barto is free from the individualism marring the contribution of the aristocrats to the cause, and mocks their belief in ordained roles. He abandons himself to the conflict at hand; and Rinaldo Guidascarpi and Carlo Ammiani, rescued amidst the street fighting in Milan, are indebted to his readiness for personal sacrifice. The hatred and fear which Barto Rizzo inspires in the aristocrats, especially Carlo Ammiani, seem like class trepidation. Carlo describes Barto as "vermin": "he fancies himself a patriot—he is only a conspirator". This distinction was commonplace in the English press, and George Eliot was dismayed by Mazzini's conspiratorial reputation. But in the opera at La Scala, Camilla (Young Italy) willingly admits to the charge of conspiracy, a necessary means of liberating her country. Leone, a volunteer under Carlo Ammiani, praises Carlo to Vittoria, but is more impressed with the resource of Barto Rizzo, also serving with the band. "We are all for Barto, though our captain Carlo is often enraged with him. But there's no getting on without him." Later, Leone remarks that "Count Ammiani has a grudge against Barto, though he can't help making use of him". One grudge is over the exposure of Vittoria's mixed loyalties, but Carlo's compromise is typically aristocratic: temporarily, distaste is subordinated to the need to "make use" of the democrat.

The insight here suggests more detachment than Meredith is able to sustain; and Barto's behaviour following the fighting in Milan is quizzically described. "In the hour of triumph Barto Rizzo had no lust for petty vengeance. The magnanimous devil plumped his gorge contentedly on victory." Here the second sentence mars the applause of the first. While Barto is shown as consistently admirable, Meredith is always prepared with the qualification: the devil is magnanimous, but still a devil. If Carlo Ammiani's limitations derive from his class nurture, Barto's are inscrutable. We hear of voraciousness in the devotion precluding "lust for petty vengeance", but the morbidity is only hinted, never defined.

Barto's wife acquiesces in the subordination to her husband which Vittoria resists when married to Carlo. The conspirator's derision of the other sex is merely a perverse generalisation from misfortune in the past: "he had been twice betrayed by women . . . he doubted the patriotism of all women". Like Carlo, however, he is susceptible to the exalted charms of Violetta d'Isorella, and undertakes the Brescian venture at her prompting. At last, his actions coincide with Meredith's denigration: capitulating to Violetta, he is also contrite before Vittoria. Actually betrayed by Pericles, Barto has ordered Vittoria's assassination in the event of his imprisonment, but adopts his wife's view that the failure of the attempt is a manifestation of divine providence. He has regressed to the vanity of fatalism, usually an aristocratic attribute. Barto admits that if Vittoria were innocent, as providence seems to indicate, "I have had two years of madness. If she is right, I was wrong; I was a devil of hell". Here Meredith confirms that Barto's was indeed "the language of a distorted mind", and we are supposed to see Vittoria as the victim of Barto's vile suspicions of her sex. But there have been grounds for suspicion in her case, and Meredith has remarked on the inadequacy of her good intentions.

The reversal of Barto's self-deprecation is inspired only by his misunderstanding Vittoria's attitude to the fight for Lombardy. He is still to be diagnosed as *"plot mad"*, the condition assigned to Mazzini by *The Times*. Meredith's failure of nerve occurs closer to the roots of the popular movement. Nevertheless, Barto's dismissal from the company of Vittoria, Carlo and his mother is curiously prim: "the hour was too full of imminent grief for either of the three to regard this scene as other than a gross intrusion ended". Viewed by Barto with "passive malice", Wilfrid Pierson is exasperated less by the look than its coming from "an Italian of the plebs". Meredith, too, is vulnerable; but Barto's dismissal from the novel coincides with his own death in the Brescian escapade in an heroic attempt to save the aristocrat, Angelo Guidascarpi. The incident is bereft of commentary: an atonement, perhaps, to the plebeian "madman" whom, however, there is no getting on without.

The portrayal of Barto Rizzo in *Vittoria* relates to that of the Chief, who appears strangely remote from the action which he instigates. Here Meredith was reflecting the lofty detachment of Mazzini's nationalism from mass needs. His creed was socially radical in its concern with the nation as a whole, emphasising equality and decrying individual privilege and aggrandisement. Mazzini was out of sympathy with *laissez-faire* economics. But he was also necessarily opposed to the socialists, who disparaged the nation and held that modes of production determined historical change. To Mazzini, their stress on state ownership seemed to preclude all that was most precious: idealism, self-sacrifice and the unique national spirit. Marx argued that a free Germany was dependent on the emancipation of the proletariat, and Mazzini that Italian workers would not be free so long as Italy was in chains. The incompatibility of nationalism with the concept of class warfare, which Barto Rizzo portends in *Vittoria*, caused the Chief to be shown as histrionic, without diminishing Mazzini's appeal to Meredith.

As possessing qualities lacking amongst the English middle class and Italian aristocracy, Meredith commends the Chief, dedicated to the republican cause and with passions "absolutely in harmony with the intelligence". Mazzini's insight as much as his devotion attracted Meredith's hero-worship. In "Europe: Its Conditions and Prospects", written in 1852 for the *Westminster Review* at the prompting of George Eliot, Mazzini claimed that Europe no longer had "unity of faith, of mission, or of aim". The

165

privileged social position of monarchy, aristocracy and monied bourgeoisie were all features of the old unity, then in its state of crisis. Through *Sandra Belloni* and *Vittoria*, Meredith shows the tendency of English society to breed individuals whose purpose in life is cloudy and imprecise. Wilfrid Pole's vagaries are typical of his class, and in *Beauchamp's Career*, Dr Shrapnel reflects Meredith's view: "the religion of this vast English middle-class ruling the land is Comfort . . . there you get at their point of unity". The middle class was sympathetic to Piedmont because Victor Emmanuel did not threaten comfort, and alarmed by Mazzini, who took into account the wants of the masses; in his own phrase, "the unchained lion", as they began to appear to their superiors. Mazzini's persuasion was that to which, in *Vittoria*, the aristocrat Carlo Ammiani is converted by experience: that the revolution's success was dependent on popular support.

Like Meredith, Swinburne revered Mazzini, and in *Lesbia Brandon*, which was begun in 1864, portrayed a republican, Count Attilio Mariani, as "admirably narrow-minded and single-hearted", like the Chief in *Vittoria*. But Swinburne makes one criticism of Mariani, and there is no suggestion that the Count, as an aristocrat, is considered a dubious adherent of Mazzini, though that he can be both is significant. "Among his few legacies, he left to Herbert Seyton two books dissimilar and incongruous enough; the Memoir of Orsini, and the *Chartreuse de Parme*. He had been likened to Palla Ferrante, and felt flattered when near his death at the comparison. Even the sublime vanity of martyrs has its weak side." Orsini was executed for his attempted assassination of Louis Napoleon. Palla Ferrante, in Stendhal's novel of 1839, has been sentenced to death as a rebel, and lives by scrupulous robbery in the woods around Parma. With a mistress and five children to support, he is smitten by the Duchess Sanseverina, who wants Ferrante to kill the Duke of Parma in return for a deed of gift in favour of his starving children. The revolutionary abhors the intrusion of material considerations; though admitting that his death would be fatal to his dependants. Ferrante's idealism, and his conviction of his importance as a natural leader, are attributes which, in *Vittoria*, Meredith shows to divide the aristocrats from the mass-movement. Angelo Guidascarpi accuses the Chief of failing to understand the feelings of aristocrats. But Swinburne is readier than Meredith to suggest that any such accusation is misconceived, and that Mazzini's nationalism was pervaded by the idealism to which the aristocrats were prone.

A. H. Clough was another who both admired and criticised Mazzini. In *Amours de Voyage*, Mazzini's rhetoric was mocked by Clough's hero Claude, an English observer in Rome in 1849, when the poem was composed:

> Sweet it may be and decorous, perhaps, for the country to die;
> but,
> On the whole we conclude the Romans won't do it, and I shan't.

Claude will, if he dies for anyone, die for the "d—— and dirty plebeians" rather than the country, still less good manners and the British female. But he cannot take the "vapour of Italy's freedom" seriously, and the tribute to Mazzini is intentionally ambiguous, praising the revolutionary for fine words:

> Honour for once to the tongue and the pen of the eloquent
> writer!
> Honour to speech! and all honour to thee, thou noble
> Mazzini!

The vaporous rhetoric is deflated by the uncompromising earthiness of the only action which Claude sees during the fight for the republic, the butchering of a priest in the streets of Rome. Though it inspired nobler action, the Mazzinian mode is still, Clough demonstrates, remote from the actualities of revolution. Claude is forced back to the eccentric pose which he finds increasingly difficult to sustain. Estranged from the class society in which he moves, he is too intelligent to overlook the limitations of Mazzini's radical alternative.

So is Meredith, but the limitations are not defined in *Vittoria*, as they are in *Amours de Voyage*. Barto Rizzo, a more engaged revolutionary than the Chief, disregards his vagaries and is a kind of touchstone: he is also, we must believe, mad. Through the Italian novels, Meredith exposes the aristocratic and middle-class tendency to idealise and practically subjugate women; but there is an instance in *Vittoria* where the novelist is guilty. A letter

addressed to Vittoria by the Chief has been passed on to her by
Carlo Ammiani:

> but how, thought Carlo, can a mind like Vittoria's find matter to
> suit her in such sentences? He asked himself the question, for-
> getting that a little time gone by, while he was aloof from the
> tumult and dreaming of it, this airy cloudy language, and every
> symbolism, had been strong sustaining food, a vital atmosphere,
> to him. He did not for the moment . . . understand that among the
> nobler order of women there is, when *they* plunge into strife, a
> craving for idealistic truths, which men are apt, under the heat and
> hurry of their energies, to put aside as stars that are meant merely
> for shining.

Mazzini's is the rhetoric of dream, and Meredith is critical,
but must qualify his criticism by finding those to whom such
sustenance is a permanent necessity, "the nobler order of women".
We have not heard before of any such order, but the invention
justifies the abstractions of Mazzini's nationalism, and this is
necessary because class fears prevent Meredith acclaiming Barto
Rizzo, the genuine social revolutionary.

Actually, Mazzini's nationalism is rejected in *Vittoria*, and
strangely, in favour of an Italy unified under the Piedmontese
monarchy. Denouncing Barto Rizzo, Carlo Ammiani remarks
that unfortunately, "the chief trusts him", and Meredith is revealed as sharing the aristocrat's nervousness of the association.
Ultimately, even Mazzini's idealism was too radical for the
novelist who was to write to John Morley in 1906, forty years
after *Vittoria*: "the list of Labour Members rejoices me in one
way, rather alarms me in another. Will they be open to large questions?" Meredith's aversion to the middle class was shared with
John Stuart Mill and the other great Liberals of the age.

Vittoria, we are told, responds bravely to the death of her
husband, Carlo Ammiani. Merthyr Powys saves her "by his
absolute trust in her fortitude to bear the great sorrow un-
deceived"; and she is compared with Italy living "through the
hours which brought her face to face with her dearest in death".
For her, too, there is consolation; and Vittoria, "on the day, ten
years later, when an Emperor and a King stood beneath the vault
of the grand Duomo, and the organ and a peel of voices rendered
thanks to Heaven for liberty, could show the fruit of her devotion

in the dark-eyed boy, Carlo Merthyr Ammiani". We have to re-member here what Meredith is inclined to gloss over in his own celebration, that the free Italy inherited by Vittoria's son is not the republic for which Mazzini fought. An Italy unified under Piedmont may be the fruit of devotion corresponding with the deepest aspirations of those after whom Vittoria's child is named: Italian aristocrat and Welsh landowning partisan. Vit-toria, though, is not an aristocrat. There is a peculiarity about the citing of Emperor and King, which evokes earlier analyses of the nature of imperialism (Austrian and English rather than French, but that should be irrelevant) and the monarchy. But any irony is out of context, and the triumph of Victor Emmanuel merits Vittoria's singing for the last time in Milan.

An earlier passage in the novel shows Meredith vacillating. Once, when Italy felt her chains, Mazzini had acted the grave leech, counting "the beating of her pulse between long pauses, that would have made another think life to be heaving its last, not beginning". Meredith considers the future which awaits the revived Italy:

> the time was coming for her to prove, by the virtues within her, that she was worthy to live, when others of her sons, subtle, and adept, intricate as serpents, bold, unquestioning as well be-stridden steeds, should grapple and play deep for her in the game of worldly strife.

Meredith does not care for the serpentine Cavour; but Italy must enter "the game of worldly strife", and serpents may be the best competitors. There enters the suggestion that Mazzini is un-worldly, at odds with his fellow-men: the view of *The Times* (criticising not Mazzini's nationalism, since he was assumed to be a socialist, but his revolutionary aspirations as such), which Meredith has already disputed. The image of Mazzini as the grave leech betrays a need to do him extravagant honour in the past, before rejecting him in the present. Many who praised Mazzini and the Roman Republic in 1849 had transferred their loyalties to Piedmont ten years later. Amelia Blandford Edward's *Half a Million of Money*, always averse to Mazzini, ends with the re-publican heroine's conversion to moderation: "she could no longer immolate herself for Italy, for the simple reason that Italy was satisfied to settle her own affairs in a quiet Constitutional way". In Meredith's novel, Vittoria is equally willing to be guided by events; though here, at least, the association of maturity with acceptance of Piedmont is incongruous. Meredith wondered what his readers would think of the omission of the "nuptial torch" in the last chapter of *Sandra Belloni*. *Vittoria*'s conclusion was conventional enough to please.

Merthyr Powys' condescension to women suggests that he, like Carlo Ammiani, is only an imagined democrat. But the Welsh landowner's devotion is steadily less qualified, until finally he is credited with "the real Divine strength" which he preaches to Vittoria, and which has previously been shown as the outstanding attribute of the Chief. Meredith had a tenderness for Celts, and liked to believe in his own Welsh ancestry. As the author becomes increasingly wary of social radicalism, Merthyr sheds his class perspective to discern and exemplify what is best in the Risorgimento. He is an assurance within the novel of Meredith's competence to write an objective history of the revolution: as we can trust Merthyr, so we can Meredith, even in his conclusion to *Vittoria*.

For once, Miss Edwards in *Half a Million of Money* improves on Meredith. Lord Castletowers, who learns better sense, begins with republican sympathies:

> on all questions of English polity, Lord Castletowers was what is somewhat vaguely called a "liberal conservative"; on all Italian subjects, a thorough-going *bonnet rouge*. He would no more have advocated universal suffrage in his own country than he would have countenanced slavery in Venetia; but he firmly believed in the possible regeneration of the great Roman republic, and avowed that belief with unhesitating enthusiasm.

It is credible that Castletowers is able to shift his allegiance to Piedmont, and while Miss Edwards approves, she is ready to admit that his Italian engagement has never been profound. He is a franker representation of the British landowner than Merthyr Powys, whose adaptability to circumstance is shared by a less complacent author. Meredith's regard for Mazzini did not preclude a more radical scepticism, though the organ and peal of voices announce a retreat to orthodoxy.

Despite himself, Meredith's conclusion to his novel of the Risor-

gimento is as characteristically English as Wilfrid Pierson's posing
during the battle. National forebodings were expressed by Wilkie
Collins in *No Name* (1862) in describing the typical inhabitant
of Lambeth, "the hideous London vagabond—with the filth of the
street outmatched in his speech, with the mud of the street out-
dirtied in his clothes . . . the public disgrace of his country, the
unheeded warning of social troubles that are yet to come". These
fears were authentic but nebulous, and the writers bent on rousing
their generation had leeway to negate their own warnings. The
historical novels of Meredith and Gaskell, as well as those of
Dickens and Eliot, sometimes descend to middle-class wish-fulfilment. With the English revolution two centuries and more comfortably in the past, a certain immutability might be assigned to
the established order, but the social troubles anticipated in the
1860s were France's immediate prehistory: the revolutions of
1789 and 1830, and those of 1848, the theme of Flaubert's
L'Education Sentimentale (1869). The idealism of the English
historical novels is obvious from the most cursory comparison with that masterpiece. If Flaubert was no more of a democrat
than his English contemporaries, he was not liable to treat the
class-conscious populace as either merely irrational or illusory.
A resuscitation of Carthage in *Salammbô* (1862) was Flaubert's
comprehensive escape from current dilemmas. The disquiet of the
English novelists was palliated by their ability finally to draw the
moral from more recent history that analysis and dread of
democracy were alike superfluous.

Select Bibliography

A. History

Ben-Israel, H. *English Historians on the French Revolution* (Cambridge, 1968).

Best, G. *Mid-Victorian Britain, 1851–75* (1971).

Blake, R. *Disraeli* (1966).

Briggs, A. and Saville, J. (ed.). *Essays in Labour History* (1967).

Dyos, H. J. and Woolf, M. *The Victorian City: Images and Realities* (1973).

Geyl, P. *Debates with Historians* (1955).

Harrison, R. *Before the Socialists* (1965).

Hobsbawm, E. J. *Labouring Men* (1964).

Saville, J. (ed.). *Democracy and the Labour Movement* (1954).

Semmel, B. *The Governor Eyre Controversy* (1962).

Smith, F. B. *The Making of the Second Reform Bill* (Cambridge, 1966).

Thompson, E. P. *The Making of the English Working Class* (Harmondsworth, 1968).

Vincent, J. *The Formation of the British Liberal Party, 1857–68* (1966).

Young, G. M. *Victorian England: Portrait of an Age* (1936).

B. Criticism

Burns, W. *Charles Reade: a Study in Victorian Authorship* (New York, 1961).

Davie, D. *The Heyday of Sir Walter Scott* (1961).

Fleishman, A. *The English Historical Novel: Walter Scott to Virginia Woolf* (1971).

Fletcher, I. (ed.). *Meredith Now* (1971).

Hardy, B. (ed.). *Critical Essays on George Eliot* (1970).

Lindsay, J. *George Meredith: His Life and Work* (1956).

Lucas, J. *The Melancholy Man: a Study of Dickens' Novels* (1970).

—— (ed.). *Literature and Politics in the Nineteenth Century* (1971).

Lukacs, G. *The Historical Novel* (1962).

Myers, W. F. T. 'Politics and Personality in *Felix Holt*', *Renaissance and Modern Studies*, X (1968) pp. 5–33.

Reynolds, G. *Victorian Painting* (1966).

Rosenburg, J. D. *The Darkening Glass: a portrait of Ruskin's genius* (1963).

Santangelo, G. A. *The Background of George Eliot's 'Romola'* (unpublished dissertation) (University of North Carolina, 1962).

Simmons, J. C. 'The Novelist as Historian: an Unexplored Tract of Victorian Historiography', *Victorian Studies*, XIV (March 1971) pp. 293–305.

Tarratt, M. *Elizabeth Gaskell's Attitude to the Art of Fiction as Revealed in her Later Work, 1855–66* (unpublished dissertation) (Oxford University, 1966).

Trilling, L. *Matthew Arnold* (1939).

Watt, I. *The Rise of the Novel* (1957).

Williams, R. *Culture and Society, 1780–1950* (1958).

—— *The Country and the City* (1973).

Index

176